The Baby Room

The Baby Room

Principles, Policy and Practice

Kathy Goouch and Sacha Powell

Open University Press

Open University Press
McGraw-Hill Education
McGraw-Hill House
Shoppenhangers Road
Maidenhead
Berkshire
England
SL6 2QL

email: enquiries@openup.co.uk
world wide web: www.openup.co.uk

and Two Penn Plaza, New York, NY 10121-2289, USA

First published 2013

A catalogue record of this book is available from the British Library

ISBN-13: 978-0-33-524636-6 (pb)
ISBN-10: 0-33-524636-2 (pb)
eISBN: 978-0-33-524637-3

Library of Congress Cataloging-in-Publication Data
CIP data applied for

Typesetting and e-book compilations by
RefineCatch Limited, Bungay, Suffolk
Printed and bound by CPI Group (UK) Ltd, Croydon, CR0 4YY

Fictitious names of companies, products, people, characters and/or data that may be used herein (in case studies or in examples) are not intended to represent any real individual, company, product or event.

The *McGraw·Hill* Companies

Contents

Acknowledgements

This book would not have been possible without the interest and support of Fiona Richman at Open University Press and we wish to thank her for her expertise and patience.

We would like to extend our thanks to all the babies who have put up with our intrusions into their baby rooms and to their families for allowing us to do so and talking to us about their babies' care. We want to shout a huge 'thank you' to the baby room practitioners who have generously given their time to the Baby Room Project since we began in 2009; to their managers and colleagues for supporting them and us; and to the Medway Advisory Team for the brilliance of their own research insights and deeply thoughtful conversations with us. These groups of dedicated and inspirational people are: Carly, Carrie, Chris, Christie, Claire, Danielle, Donna, Emma, Heather, Jo, Karen, Kelly, Leanne, Leeanne, Lisa, Louise, Louise, Mel, Nikki, Rachel, Radka, Roxy, Samme, Sarah, Sarah-Jayne, Stacey, Tessa, Tracey, and Vicky (practitioners); Kirsteen, Anita, Carley, Chris, Clare, Emma, Gill, Judith, Karen, Lesley, Lucy, Patsy, Pauline, Susie, Tracey, and Victoria (advisors).

In addition, our work with the project groups has been richly supplemented by the companionship of several wise people who agreed to dedicate many hours of their time as members of our Expert Group and to whom we are deeply indebted. They are: Liz Attenborough, Laura Barbour, Jo Baranek, Tricia David, Peter Elfer, Janet Moyles, Helen Moylett, Jools Page, and Liz Roberts.

We wish to thank the Esmée Fairbairn Foundation for their faith in us, and the funding they provided to enable the project to happen over two successive phases. Their belief in the importance of babies' daycare is a testament to the integrity and breadth of thinking of the Foundation concerning the concept of education.

We would also like to say thank you to our long-distance colleagues in China, the USA, Scotland, the Republic of Ireland, the Netherlands, and New Zealand for providing other lenses on our research and to our colleagues at Canterbury Christ Church University for their interest, encouragement, and belief in the value of the Baby Room Project work.

And finally: (From Sacha) With love and thanks to Beanie, Eliot, Nathan and Sebastian (my babies), Dave and the wonderful people who have cared for all of us. I'd like to say a very special thanks to 'Nana' (what goes around comes around) and to K (the best kind of company to keep). (From Kathy) I owe special thanks to my wise and attendant husband Brian, and to Gill and Joe whose babyhoods I will never forget. And in memory of my mother, who knew about babies.

Foreword

Tricia David

Most poets know that poetry is grounded in the earliest experiences, in memory too deep to name, stored in the senses rather than in the filing-system of the conscious mind. It is upon those feelings and experiences at the wellspring of language, where words are newborn, that the poet needs to draw . . . To go back as far as the source, where what is 'real' and what is imagined, what comes from lullaby, nursery rhyme or fairy story, and the white noise of the world . . . is all tangled up . . . It is the pure spirit of language. There the human being is brand new. Words store and offer back our memories . . . 'Nothing is until it has a word'.

(Clarke, 2008)

When we were babies in the womb, we eavesdropped on the sounds of our mothers' lives, their own voices and those of others, the tunes of the languages they spoke, the tunes they were surrounded by. Once living in the outer world, we continued to listen and to try to make sense of the different sounds, and to use the languages of our family and community. How words are used impacts on those with whom we come into contact, whether baby, child, adolescent or adult.

In this book, Kathy and Sacha have thoughtfully reported on their Baby Room Project, using carefully selected words, to provide insights, to challenge assumptions, and to help us engage in meaningful debates about how our society thinks of and treats babies and the staff of baby rooms, who offer them care and learning experiences. Sometimes English, for all its roots and richness, does not have a word for what we mean – 'care and education'; 'teachers who are carers' . . .

Recently, Ann Langston (2012) drew attention to the importance of Professor Lesley Abbott's seminal and key foundation document, *Birth to Three Matters* (DfES, 2002), superseded by the introduction of the Early Years Foundation Stage (DCSF, 2008). Compiling the background review of relevant literature (David et al., 2003) for *Birth to Three Matters*, we were initially some-what shocked to realize the extent to which the earliest years in children's lives had been neglected by education and early years researchers – though not by developmental psychologists. We were also initially challenged by the idea of trying to categorize the information for the review into the 'Aspects', namely: a strong child; a skilful communicator; a competent learner; and a healthy child. However, we soon recognized that the Aspects would overlap to no greater extent than the 'old' system borrowed from psychology (physical; emotional; social and cognitive development) and that this thoughtful way of focusing on children's growing capabilities would make more sense for our field. At the same time, it seemed more respectful towards babies and young children as 'whole' people.

During the years since *Birth to Three Matters*, Kathy Goouch and Sacha Powell became increasingly determined to continue researching this area, especially as children from birth to 3 years were now – at last – becoming recog-nized as human beings capable of thinking, communicating, and learning. However, as Kathy and Sacha note in this book, the new acknowledgement of the tremendously active brains of the very young was only part of the story. More mothers were returning to work earlier than they would have done in the past and out-of-home care has been expanding.

Funded by the Esmée Fairbairn Foundation, Kathy and Sacha were fortu-nate to find nursery settings and staff working in the field who were willing to join them in investigating the who, what, how, and why of baby rooms and this book reports in detail on the facts, processes, and dilemmas which came to light. Without the loyal participation of these workers and their managers, the project could not have been undertaken. Their story, as told in this book, is an important account of the building of a trusting and supportive network.

Participation in the project

Other participants in the project, while never having access to sensitive or confidential data from the main threads, wove in and around the glorious tapestry this work constitutes. There were international contacts; interested colleagues in other parts of the UK eager to become involved in their own baby room projects; and a group of us known as 'the expert panel' (though for my own part I have always denied being an expert in anything because I am so aware of the enormity of my ignorance). Besides, this is one area where few people know very much, because baby rooms and baby room staff have been neglected, isolated, and hidden. Thankfully, as a result of the project we now know more, although further research is needed in this complex field.

Ethical research considerations

All research concerned with human beings is subjected to scrutiny in relation to research ethics. Every stage of the process must ensure participants are treated respectfully, informed about the aims of the research and of their right to withdraw at any time. Clearly, where babies and young children are involved, the researchers are required to be sensitive to any child's reaction to their presence – a form of acquiring consent – and to have obtained parental consent for them to be included. Similarly, the consent of all adults involved must be sought. Furthermore, since researchers would usually be construed as more powerful than participants, they must be sensitive to this issue and its implications.

Clearly, when a book grows out of a project, one needs to be aware of the ways in which participants may view and interpret publication. It is, after all, a document in which parts of their lives are exposed (even when a project is underpinned by strict principles of anonymity and confidentiality) and which they may feel does, or does not, do them justice.

Kathy and Sacha spent much time reflecting and being reflexive about ethical issues, which were often raised at our panel sessions, frequently followed by suggestions of further, thought-provoking readings.

Complexity and volume of the data generated

Members of the panel were often struck by the ambitious scope of the work and the enormous quantity and complexity of data being generated. Kathy and Sacha have combed and re-combed their material, discussed their thoughts with the participants and their managers, and at panel meetings. As a result, the report contained in this book provides the field of ECEC – practitioners, parents, policy-makers, and researchers – with much that we in England need to debate, not least the apparently widespread understanding that the practitioners themselves felt their views on policy did not count. Interestingly, this was a view we found a decade ago when exploring approaches to early literacy (David et al., 2000). Given the chance and situations in which they feel confident and respected, as here, baby room staff show they are competent and articulate about what matters to them.

While bringing its own contemporary messages to the field, this study of baby rooms has built on the small but important body of work about babies and their experiences. It follows earlier studies in the UK, such as those by John and Elizabeth Newson, Penny Leach, Judy Dunn, Elinor Goldschmied, Sonia Jackson, Brian Jackson, Peter Elfer, Dorothy Selleck, Colwyn Trevarthen, Lesley Abbott, Rosie Roberts, Cathy Nutbrown, Jools Page, and Julia Manning-Morton, by not only challenging thinking and assumptions but also linking theory, research, and practice in deeply thoughtful dialogues.

Learning from the Baby Room Project

Perhaps each of us will take away from this study something personal about trying to understand baby rooms from the perspective of babies themselves. The centrality of relationships, the issue of how we ensure each baby feels cherished wherever they happen to be, means reflecting on aspects such as continuity of contact between babies and their key persons (as well as with any siblings or friends who also attend the setting), and the quality of the relationship between staff and a baby's family.

So who is rocking the cradle? Asking questions and reflecting on the responses

The title chosen by Kathy and Sacha for the first chapter in this book – *The baby room: who is rocking the cradle?* – asks a question. The old saying, 'The hand that rocks the cradle rules the world' is surely a warning to us to think carefully what we wish for, what we plan and provide, how we model ways of being. We are born to be social, to enjoy warm interaction, touch and shared endeavour. The baby room staff who participated in this project were clearly aware that the babies in their care came with these capacities – but to what extent are they appropriately supported at nursery, local, and national levels in rocking the cradle?

1 The baby room
Who is rocking the cradle?

The title of this introductory chapter was suggested by an article on the work of evolutionary biologists, which claims that while 'traditionally child-rearing was guided by patriarchal ideas', the situation is changing and perhaps now 'the cradle rocks to an older rhythm' (Johnson, 2012: 38). It may be that this optimism is premature, that patriarchal ideas and policies still prevail, or at least lurk in the shadows, but the exploration of history and power in relation to the care of children, and babies in particular, is timely. How babies and very young children are being cared for, both inside and outside of the home, has begun to take centre stage in England, as it has in many countries around the world, as the significance of very high-profile research and key policy debates circles around women and children. While the economic value of education is frequently promoted and valued simply as 'a producer of labour and skills' (Ball, 2008: 11), economic arguments also play a central role in debates about formal arrangements for childcare, as for some decades women have had access to an increasing slice of the labour market and care has moved from domestic to commercial contexts. The inclusion of more women in the workforce has inevitably also led to greater concern about parity in terms of pay and conditions of work, with talk of a 'motherhood penalty' in the UK (Ben-Galim, 2011: 7). The role of the state has changed, and is changing, in determining how women fit in a contemporary labour market, particularly in determining:

- the critical increase and regulations surrounding part-time employment;
- the financial relationships with parents and providers for childcare costs and support;
- the levels of intervention that the state will provide to protect and enrich the development, education, and health of babies, particularly in areas of so-called disadvantage.

The combined field of early childhood education and care (ECEC) has become increasingly interesting to governments, including the British government, as they seek to address a number of issues relating to child poverty, welfare reforms, social mobility, and work patterns for women and mothers (Allen, 2011; Field, 2010). Increasingly, where care is concerned, the arguments relate to the economic case for expanding childcare provision (Ben-Galim, 2011). As families' economic situations are shifting, with employment downturns and the need to readjust working arrangements, inevitably patterns of childcare change. Alongside this, social attitudes towards family practices in relation to who cares for young children and child-rearing practices in general are also undergoing change, as more babies under the age of 2 years, in the UK but also elsewhere (Organization for Economic Cooperation and Development (OECD), 2006), are cared for by people who are not members of their family. Such changes are taking place within the new extended parental leave context in England, and some other countries, where governments are supporting leave of up to 12 months, although at varying rates of remuneration (see OECD, 2011). Surveys report that most women with young children in Europe would rather be in full-time employment if they had a 'quality child care solution' (OECD, 2006). However, preferences about childcare types in England have been found to vary according to the child's age, whether mothers were asked before or after childbirth, and in relation to their circumstances on both occasions (Barnes et al., 2006). Childcare is an expensive commodity and it seems that, in England in particular, formal childcare is becoming so costly that it now forms a major part of families' expenditure, with much of the provision emanating from the private sector (Alderman and Vegas, 2011). This shift in family practices is not restricted to the poorest families in any sense. In spite of apparent increased public expenditure on children's services in recent years, the UK still performs poorly in childcare scales in relation to the Nordic countries, and 'significant shortcomings' are said to exist especially for services for children under 3 years of age (OECD, 2006: 104). This is reported to be due to an unforeseen number of women in the workforce and the national government's response to this, which has been a heavy reliance on the private sector. In addition, with new UK government initiatives to ensure that 2-year-olds from disadvantaged families have a 15-hour free entitlement to nursery education, an already stretched service is presented with new challenges. However, issues of quality in relation to the speed of growth of this sector are yet to be resolved.

In contemporary western countries, assumptions are made that provision for babies and very young children to be cared for outside of the home will exist. However, the ensuing regulations, relationships, and interventions at state level all come at a considerable cost. Current political imperatives and resultant policies in relation to both education and care indicate a more complete move towards a business model with the potential consequence that profit, competition, and market forces will themselves create a level of quality that can be purchased, as a service, by working parents. Regulations exist to monitor standards of quality, although how in practice these are enacted and experienced remains problematic.

There appear to be competing discourses relating to formal daycare for babies, in the areas of research, provision, and public policy. Some research makes claims for formal daycare in relation to avoidance of risk to babies (Cuthbert et al., 2011) and better educational outcomes and challenge to social disadvantage (EACEA, 2009; Sammons et al., 2004; Siraj-Blatchford and Sylva, 2004). However, there are counterclaims from research indicating potential damage to children from being within daycare systems (James, 2010; Kottelenberg and Lehrer, 2011). Public policy, while promoting the notions of 'women into work' and 'make work pay', appears to be avoiding issues of the logistics of childcare and is instead directing the public gaze towards potential beneficial outcomes linking to educational gains and ultimately 'school readiness'. The third discourse relates to provision and here there are tensions from within and outside the practice field. For example, there are a number of stakeholders involved in monitoring practice. These include government agencies, such as Ofsted (the Office for Standards in Education, Children's Services and Skills), as well as business investors and families. It is easy to understand where such tensions, for example in relation to expenditure and quality, may exist. Within practice, the care of under 2s does not attract government funding in the UK and therefore it is frequently the case that the least qualified members of staff are employed with this age group, who themselves feel neglected and overlooked in relation to training and professional development in general (Goouch and Powell, 2012). In view of the existence of this apparently hidden situation in the UK in relation to formal daycare for babies, the conflicting aims of various 'stakeholders' and the challenges of the current financial climate for women, parents, and families, we ask the following questions:

- Should 'baby rooms' exist?
- What and who are they for, and who seeks to benefit from them?
- What are the philosophical, political, and pedagogical frameworks within which formal daycare for babies is located?
- What kinds of care and/or educational/developmental opportunities do they provide and why?
- What can we learn about societal values, principles, and practices compared with those of other nations?
- What are the implications for babies in daycare?

These questions indicate research interests that span disciplines, including philosophical challenges when asking about the very existence of care outside the family as well as socio-political challenges in determining whose interests are primarily being served and whose have been relegated in the process. In addition, while currently provision in England has much in common with that of some other English-speaking countries, its stated aims and practices for babies and young children remain far removed from that of some European nations.

While the debates continue, in political, policy, and academic circles, approximately 42 per cent of babies receive care outside of their home in the UK, some informally by family members and others in daycare settings. There has been little research undertaken in relation to the nature of the care of babies in formal daycare settings, although much has been written about child development and brain development, and there are some essential research texts dealing with national and international policies in relation to childcare practices (e.g. Dahlberg and Moss, 2005; Gammage, 2006, 2008; OECD 2006, 2012; UNICEF, 2008). It seems that the picture of 'baby rooms' in nurseries, where babies sometimes as young as 6 weeks are being cared for, is determined by a somewhat fragmented if not completely hidden discourse that surrounds decisions made about the out-of-home care of infants. This discourse often appears to centre on the balance between the earning power of women and the affordability of care. One side of the argument makes a case for universal child-care, claiming economic benefits for society in general:

> On the basis of new cost–benefit analysis, we show that universal childcare pays a return to the government of £20,050 (over four years) in terms of tax revenue minus the cost of childcare for every woman who returns to full-time employment after one year of maternity leave. We therefore argue that the provision of universal child-care should be a strategic priority for public service and welfare reform in the UK.
>
> (Ben-Galim, 2011: 2)

At the same time, others argue that daycare provision for infants and young children is becoming unaffordable, making the economic argument unbalanced and rather contentious in a new climate of political direction to 'make work pay' and in an international context where, in the report below, the cost of childcare in England is claimed to be among the most expensive in the world:

> The survey findings suggest that parents living in severe poverty are struggling to access childcare more than other parents, particularly due to the high cost. This is undermining the UK government's laudable aim to make work pay, and thus preventing families living on the lowest incomes from escaping poverty.
>
> (Save the Children/Daycare Trust, 2012: 1)

Furthermore, there are some who maintain that the long debated claims of research into attachment by Bowlby – 'This whole business of mothers going to work, it's so bitterly controversial, but I do not think it's a good idea' (Bowlby, 1989, cited in Johnson, 2012) – are relevant today (James, 2010; Kottelenberg and Lehrer, 2011). The debates driving the expansion of child-care are complex and in England, as in other countries, the solutions are diverse, variously motivated, unevenly funded, and differently supported. Although governments are making powerful economic arguments, relevant and challenging at both macro and family levels as above, and devising policy on these bases, social science researchers, educationalists, and neuroscientists are presenting the case differently:

> The research literature confirms the benefits of formal early child-hood education for three and four-year-olds and for children from disadvantaged families. However, the evidence is not so clear for infants and toddlers except to demonstrate that 'quality' is at the centre of all issues relating to the attendance of under 2s in formal ECS. In other words, whether the substitution of parental care for non-parental care results in an increase or decrease in child well-being depends on the quality of the care, because high quality early childhood education and care is a key predictor for positive outcomes for young children.
>
> (Carroll-Lind, 2011: 40)

This report, from New Zealand, further describes the potential 'risks' to infants' and toddlers' development through long durations in education and care services, including a risk of 'disrupted attachment' through the experience of multiple carers In formal services and greater exposure to infection at a time when immune systems are underdeveloped.

Alternatively, there is a strong body of research (from an organization that seeks solutions to a globalized economy) reported to be 'unanimous' in demonstrating that there are significant benefits to the provision of early childhood care services for the child, the family, and the state:

> The major domains that benefit are: the national economy (higher employment rates and a broader tax base); health (better mental and physical health for children and families, less at-risk behaviours, family violence and emergency room visits, better fertility control); social services and criminal justice (less dependency of families on social welfare; less criminal activity among parents, higher earnings); education (better integration into primary school, better grade progression, less participation in special education).
>
> (Bennett, 2003: 36)

There is a substantial body of research from across disciplines acknowledging that the first months and years are crucial to babies' development and learning, that babies thrive when experiencing stable, loving, and stimulating relationships, and that the early stage of brain growth from birth requires experiences, interactions, and encounters to influence development. This perspective has dominated the rationales for policies and practice and yet, in spite of these findings, there is limited research into the processes and practices of group daycare for babies from birth to 2 even though the sector is growing rapidly and increasing numbers of babies are being cared for in this way.

What is known in relation to formal daycare is that there are economic and political as well as social drivers for the provision of out-of-home care for babies, for recent education and care policy developments in England, and for comparative references to other countries' provisions. It is now timely to interrogate closely how the care of babies is understood as governments examine the qualifications of those employed in the sector and measures of its quality; as the number of people seeking daycare for babies is increasing; as greater expectations are imposed on early years provision generally in relation to 'school readiness'; as the market (the baby care business) expands before issues of quality are addressed and the aims for the sector have been established; and as financial pressures on women to return to work increase in challenging times. Furthermore, in a changing world climate where austerity and constraining financial circumstances are having wide-ranging impacts, the research lens needs to incorporate the local response in relation to the international landscape in order to provide a better perspective on how different countries are demonstrating interest in, supporting or funding formal daycare for babies. What is happening in the countries of the UK needs to be viewed against the international backcloth of the economic and the care and education policy landscape. The ways in which policy frames or excludes the provision of daycare in economy-driven, market-driven, target-driven, performative-centred, and globalized societies may reflect how the status of women, families, and babies is defined and valued and how their intentions and family values are best served.

If assumptions prevail that daycare for babies should exist, a critical examination of public discourses, family values, the cultural contexts of babies' development, and the relationship between these is required. Additionally, with a continuum of research and international polemic stretching from universal daycare provision at one end to no formal daycare for babies under 2 years, questions also need to be raised about the level of (affordable and accessible) choices available for parents, mothers, and families, of different social classes and different cultures and communities. There is no doubt that as well as being a growth business in the past decade across the world, childcare is also currently a highly contested area in political and societal terms. Who looks after babies, for what purposes, towards what outcomes, and at what costs are questions that span a range of research domains as well as impacting on politics and policy creation across fields other than education and social care. For example, political decisions relating to jobs and employment, families, transport costs, and infrastructure frequently create reciprocal impacts on the field of childcare and the care of babies. Contemporary policies in different international contexts determining parental leave, maternity and paternity cover, bear related costs that are far reaching in both economic and social terms.

In this book, we do not argue for or against baby rooms in nursery provision. We instead seek to open the doors of those rooms so that we can view and understand the nature of the 'enclosures' (Dahlberg and Moss, 2005) provided for babies; view and understand who is caring for babies and how; and view and understand the environments and resources provided for their care. It is in this context – as explorers – that we began our research to collect narratives from inside baby rooms. We also sought to examine policy narratives in relation to babies' care in out-of-home contexts and to draw on international research and policy in this very specific phase of early childhood care and education. Throughout the project, with the generous support of those involved in the research process, we began to develop our own narrativized understandings.

This book is based on a research and development project carried out in South East England – the Baby Room Project – that attempted to uncover some of the practices, attitudes, and qualifications of those working with the youngest children in formal daycare settings in order to form a more complete picture of how the lives of some of these babies and the practitioners looking after them are lived. The Baby Room Project is introduced and described in Chapter 2. There we highlight the research framework on which the book rests and from which illustrative evidence is drawn. However, the critical ecological approach we have adopted demands we include debates that extend beyond the immediate contexts of this project, and some wide-ranging national reforms will be considered to support both those employed in this phase and the babies themselves – whose care, safety, development, and potential we believe can, in the best circumstances, be enriched by daycare. This book is an attempt to provide information about the range of research in relation to babies' development and care that could inform the kinds of practice that will nourish and support babies and very young children in daycare settings. It will examine the existing requirements for 'qualified' practitioners in this phase, both in England and elsewhere in the world, and will discuss the tension between the need for high-quality, regulated provision with associated qualifications and dependency on an independent, privately funded sector to make such provision. Concerns will be raised that, as already stated, frequently the least experienced and qualified practitioners are often placed in 'baby rooms' in nurseries and that these, predominantly young women feel themselves to be neglected. A key element will centre upon the notion of professionalism, including definitions of this term and implications for policy and for practice. The broader context for this will be discussed in political and policy terms, including women's employment, encouragement of market forces to dictate provision, and that provision is generally premised on its position as childcare rather than education, with the accompanying view that regulation in settings not perceived as 'education' may be weaker.

Throughout this book, we create links between theory and research and the themes and issues emanating from the project and our encounters with practice and practitioners. In Chapter 3, Baby Care Professionals, we look critically at the national context of education and care, its structures and systems, and consider the training, experience, and contexts for learning of those who work as 'practitioners' in formal daycare for babies. Chapter 4 looks at the first of three of the themes identified in the Baby Room Project and attempts to unravel the complex patterns of relationships at work in daycare settings. Included among these is that of 'key person' and research relating to this role will be examined. Chapter 5 focuses on talk, another of the central themes from the project and ranges across the complex web of talk domains in relation to babies in daycare settings. Chapter 6 has as its focus the third key theme to be examined. This chapter looks critically at how environmental factors can be limiting, constraining or 'rich' for babies who sometimes spend many hours of their early lives in these out-of-home settings, and also explores some of the issues around the problem of how environments are measured and judged. Chapter 7 begins to deconstruct some of the perspectives employed in relation to research, policy, and practice. Some insights into the impact of varying 'paradigms' on how babies and their needs are constructed are developed in this chapter. In Chapter 8, contexts of influence for both the babies and practitioners who care for them are the focus and a critical adaptation of an ecological model will be applied to support the analysis of the factors that shape experiences and relationships. International policy and politics, as they relate to practice with babies, will be examined and considered in ideological terms in Chapter 9. The final chapter, Chapter 10, attempts to draw together the theoretical perspectives and the empirical research from the Baby Room Project to identify critical themes. It makes recommendations for professional development for those working with babies and creates implications for future research and debate.

And finally

In our preparation for this book, we were struck by the many, sometimes rather entrenched, positions, across paradigms and political divides, taken by those with an interest in the early childhood field of study and politics, each it seems with clear and worthwhile agendas and with projected outcomes for the economic and social welfare of nations. However, throughout the Baby Room Project and woven intrinsically through the pages of this book are two very strongly held beliefs of our own. The first, closely interrogated in Chapter 4 but evident throughout, relates to the core finding from *Birth to Three Matters: A Review of the Literature* (David et al., 2003) that people matter to babies as they grow, develop and learn, and they do this best in the company of familiar people who love them. Being with people who are committed to them as individuals and who care what happens to them is not a luxury extra for babies but a prerequisite for their human growth. In Johnson's words, 'each and every baby has to develop thought and language for herself. Such wonderful abilities do not just appear like an instant meal pre-packed by our genes. What genes give us is the equipment to benefit from experience in such a way that language and thought become possible' (Hobson, 2002: 3). The experiences that Johnson claims to be integral to these developments centre on babies' observation and participation guided by 'a natural responsiveness' to others. He explains that babies' 'perception of others is not like their perception of cars or buildings. Being affected by others is a design feature of human beings – a design feature that transforms what a human being is' (p. 77). We know definitively from international research how important 'affectionate companionship' (Trevarthen et al., 2003: 31) is in the lives of babies, and throughout our lives.

The second thread is also explicitly examined later in the book and concerns Mouffe's (2000) notion of 'agonistic pluralism', which Moss (2008: 12–13) reasserts in the arena of ECEC politics as a means to encourage critical exchanges among 'adversaries' whose passions are retained as they seek more democratic designs. His plea reminds us of the call Tricia David made in 1995 during a speech at the University of the Sorbonne that all those of us with an interest in ECEC should enter into

> . . . a debate in which we try to develop our understanding of each other's allegiances rather than a 'paradigm war'. After all, we advocate loving acceptance of the strengths each child brings to an early years setting – are we unable to extend the same kind of respect to each other?
>
> (David, 1996: 2)

It is easy to become lost in paradigmatic debates but, in the same way that we argue for dialogic opportunities for those engaged in the care of babies and young children, so we use this opportunity to call for open dialogic exchange between researchers, between research and politics, between research, politics, and business. In this way, through dialogue, as Moss (2008) argues, there may be hope for a different approach, 'not the prospect of finding the one true way, but the possibility of finding many ways to many truths' (p. 20).

2 The Baby Room Project[1]

Introduction

Daycare for babies and young children is big business, with much of the world's daycare provision based in the private sector (Alderman and Vegas, 2011). As already stated, in England, many babies under 18 months of age spend time in formal (group) daycare settings, usually in dedicated 'baby rooms' with a key person designated as their primary caregiver (Powell and Goouch, 2012). The cost of this service is normally borne by the baby's parent(s). The provision is governed by a national, statutory framework of learning, development, and welfare requirements (DCSF, 2008), which continues in a new, revised form (DfE, 2012) and is assessed by a national inspection body, Ofsted. Local authorities offer advisory services and training, and an array of statutory and voluntary agencies may also provide an input. The system allows for a multitude of voices to declare an interest in what constitutes 'appropriate' 'good', 'best', 'high-quality' care for each baby. The plurality of perspectives opens up possibilities for contradiction, complexity, uncertainty, and confusion. In the midst of this mêlée are the babies and the people who work in the baby rooms. Predominantly, parents in England foot the bill for their babies' formal childcare, much of which is based in the private sector following a rapid marketization of provision encouraged by the former New Labour government (Penn, 2008). Daycare providers are located within the state-maintained, private and independent/voluntary sectors but a charge to parents for childcare is levied across all sectors of provision. An annual survey of childcare provision in England revealed that around 57 per cent of working families in England with a child under 1 year of age had used at least one form of (out-of-home) childcare in 2009, and this increased to 70 per cent when the child was aged 1–2 years (Smith et al., 2010). Exploring maternity and paternity rights, Chanfreau et al. (2011) found that 55 per cent of mothers who were employed prior to childbirth took no more than 39 weeks' maternity leave in 2008 and 51 per cent were using some formal childcare when they returned to work. But the percentages of mothers who used only formal childcare for their babies increased in line with hourly income (19 per cent of those earning less than £5 per hour; 46 per cent of those earning more than £20 per hour). These parents face some of the highest childcare costs in the world, with an average expenditure of £97 per week for 25 hours of childcare for a child under 2 years (Save the Children/Daycare Trust, 2012), rising significantly in cities and in London in particular.

The project

The Baby Room Project had an overarching aim to examine and influence the quality of care in out-of-home provision for babies from birth to 12 months in day nurseries. In this project, the term 'quality' refers to the standards of professionals' knowledge and understanding of babies' needs within the context of formal daycare, including the partnerships with other significant adults, and in the translation of this enhanced knowledge into skilful, attentive, and reflective practice. In addition, the project sought to raise awareness of the professional needs of those working with babies in daycare in regional, national, and international contexts. A key element of the work has been the use of original research to enable the provision of bespoke professional development sessions, offering opportunities for practitioners to reflect on their knowledge, consider how this relates to their practice, and to extend their knowledge and understanding through discussion and reflection. Frequently encountered anecdotal evidence, from across the country and gathered through our own professional and academic networks, suggests that practitioners with the least experience and qualifications are often placed in the baby rooms of daycare and nursery settings with the most qualified and experienced practitioners working with the older children. Indeed, recent research by the Daycare Trust, which sought to 'identify the elements of high quality early childhood education and care provision' and explore the associated costs, recommended that only one-third of the staff caring for children under 2 should be graduates, compared with half of staff caring for children aged 2 years and over (Daycare Trust, 2009). While this research seeks to improve the quality of care in the early years, its recommendations fail to acknowledge the importance of the knowledge and understanding that we assert is required to provide the best possible care for babies. During the Baby Room Project term (2009–2012), Professor Cathy Nutbrown was commissioned by the Department for Education to undertake an independent review of Early Education and Childcare Qualifications. Professor Nutbrown's final report has now been published (*Foundations for Quality*, 2012a). However, in the context of the project, it is important to note that in England, as elsewhere (for example, New Zealand), evaluations of the nature of the qualifications and the numbers of qualified practitioners per setting are both being reviewed by governments during a time of world recession and international financial crisis.

At the time of the project's genesis, however, clear research evidence was necessary, in a fast-changing policy and practice landscape in England, to either validate or challenge anecdotal evidence and suggest possible development pathways. The Baby Room Project has explored the potential for developing networks of support, specific training needs, and links to higher education for baby care workers. The research evidence from the OECD (2006) suggests that higher qualifications lead to 'better outcomes' for children and current government policy for workforce development has taken seriously these findings. However, the Baby Room Project also aimed to investigate the ways in which the ethos of a setting, internal support and supervision practices, as well as individuals' experiential knowledge and aspirations relating to outcomes for babies, may impact upon the 'quality' of care.

The methodology of the project

The Baby Room Project had an overarching aim to improve the quality of care in out-of-home provision for babies from birth to 12 months, specifically in day nurseries. Quality as already stated refers to the standards of professionals' knowledge and understanding of babies' developmental needs within the contexts of formal daycare, including partnerships with other significant adults such as parents and other carers, and to the translation of enhanced knowledge into skilful, attentive, and reflective practice. A series of linked objectives underpinned the project's overarching aim:

1   To offer professional development activities to enhance the knowledge and understanding of practitioners working in 'baby rooms' in ten day-care settings in socio-economically deprived parts of Kent.
2   To develop a sustainable network of practitioners who were able to provide mutual support and opportunities to reflect on a wide range of individual and shared experiences and their outcomes for babies.
3   To undertake collaborative research to:
     • better understand the factors that support or hinder the professional development of the staff who care for very young children;
     • explore the effects of professional development on practice;
     • identify the project's benefits as perceived by the participating practitioners, their colleagues and managers;
     • assess the outcomes for babies of changes in professional practice that practitioners and their managers believe to have resulted from participation in the project.

4   To disseminate the project's findings to relevant professional and academic networks, and local and national early years policy-makers.

The project's design consisted of a hybrid of research and development activities and sources of evidence, including:

- semi-structured interviews with participants and their managers;
- video-recorded, naturalistic observations of the participants' work in their baby rooms;
- interviews with the parents of a sample of babies for whom the participants were the designated key person;
- facilitated group discussions based on extracts from policy texts, media reports, videos or research findings; and
- unsolicited discussions on the project's online social networking site (the Baby Room 'NING', see below).

Data from early interviews and observations informed the structure and content of the professional development sessions and provided a 'baseline' of data against which the researchers (and evaluator) were able to explore change over the course of the project. Professional development sessions were designed and each followed a similar half-day format involving:

- informal 'welcome' time;
- reading aloud children's literature (books for babies) and deconstructing the stories;
- summarized evidence from research and implications for practice (with a different focus for each session);
- guided reflection and discussion time;
- the use of the NING or folders to document issues from the session;
- sandwich lunch and informal chat;
- follow-up activities to be undertaken between sessions (in the setting/ using the NING).

An online social network was created for the project. While originally membership of this 'NING' had been restricted to the project participants and the researchers with the intention of creating a safe, bespoke networking space for spontaneous communication in the gaps between the professional development events, this has now been extended. The participants still retain a closed site on the NING but other members have joined, with the current membership now close to a hundred. The NING has provided a resource for posting discussion prompts or questions, links to other sites (e.g. Talk to Your Baby and Nursery World), events (such as the professional development sessions and the Baby Room conferences), evaluative comments, and an email facility. The ways in which the practitioners have engaged with the NING (the frequency and content of their postings and comments) and the project folders have provided further evidence for the research, with the participants' informed and ongoing consent.

While our intention has been to develop a synergistic mosaic of evidence, this has only partially been systematically pre-planned in the sense that we were aware of the potential sources of evidence (e.g. the NING or the professional development sessions) at the design stage of the project but were unable to predict the extent to which these might or might not prove to be valuable. However, we have also found that the cumulative nature of this approach has been extremely useful in helping to develop a more 'rounded' as well as a developing picture of our own and the practitioners' learning over time. Therefore, the use of the structured (i.e. pre-planned) data collection methods supplemented by *ad hoc* sources has been beneficial overall. We have been guarded against inflated claims of causality but have included examples of impact that participants or their managers have attributed to the project.

Participation in the project

In September 2009, a group of practitioners from ten daycare settings in southeast England joined the Baby Room Project and in January 2011 the group was extended. Overall, 43 settings have been directly involved, with 21 practitioners and their settings forming the core project research and development groups. All but two of these were privately owned and all complied with the government's requirement to be registered with Ofsted as a provider of ECEC under the guidance of the statutory Early Years Foundation Stage (EYFS) (DCSF, 2008; DfE, 2012) framework for the learning and development of children from birth to 5 years. The 21 women ranged in age from 18 to 60 years with most between 18 and 25 years. They worked in baby rooms of different shapes and sizes, some with numerous colleagues, others with one or even none, and in total 360 babies spent time in their baby rooms each week. Each had responsibility as key person for at least three babies with the maximum being eight over the course of a week. All held a relevant early years or childcare qualification, mostly National Vocational Qualifications at Level 2 or 3. Although many (but not all) reported that they had accessed some in-service training or professional development during the previous couple of years, for most this training related to practical health and safety issues, food safety, child protection or safeguarding. Many worked very long hours with infrequent, short breaks and some worked in near or total isolation from colleagues caring for older children. In one case, a participant reported spending many hours alone in her baby room with occasional

'glances' through a window from her manager. The opportunities for professional dialogue were rare or non-existent and they relished the chance to
engage with other practitioners during the project's 'development sessions'.
In interviews, when asked 'What kinds of professional development
opportunities would you like to have?', one practitioner in September 2009
responded:

> I'd really like to talk to other practitioners and share our views and
> practice. Often we don't have the opportunity to go on courses
> and when we do there's not really any chance to discuss things, you
> don't get to find out what other people do or how they do this
> and that.

Another in May 2010 stated:

> I've really liked the group discussion and I always feel that the
> time seems to be over so fast; I wish we could carry on for longer.
> Sometimes it seems like we're just getting talking and then it's time to
> go and I feel like, 'Oh I wish we had longer!' There's no one particular
> thing I've enjoyed more than others but it's been really nice to talk
> about different people's things and their approaches. There's no right
> or wrong and even though some of the things we do are quite similar,
> and we might agree about something, we do have different ideas as
> well. I really enjoy the face-to-face parts.

The practitioners' reflections, documented on the NING, sometimes led to
new discussions or added to ongoing debates. The quote below originated in a
comment by one practitioner ('Lucy') during a professional development
session, which was subsequently picked up in discussion in the NING. It was
revived and extended by the practitioners at the next professional development session (which deliberately focused on relationships).

> I can't believe we are halfway through either! Time really does fly!
> It was very interesting and surprising hearing the comments from
> 'Lucy' regarding her feelings about cuddling the babies and giving
> them kisses while they are in our care. To me it is one of the pleasures
> of the job, getting to know the babies, caring for them and you
> do come to love them in some ways (no replacement for parents
> but we do have a lot of time with lots of them who are 'full-timers'
> and in my opinion become part of their primary carers). To me,
> and having spoken to my colleagues, it is a big part of the care
> to provide love for the babies and giving them cuddles when
> they need/want them. It is not something that is discouraged in

my setting and I think that most parents are pleased and reassured that their babies are receiving lots of love and care while they are with us.

(NING entry, January 2010)

The above comment, written in January 2010, was an early example of unsolicited use of the NING by the practitioners. The NING is divided into different sections. The discussion board allows members to initiate and reply to discussions at any time. Between October and December 2009, there were just three responses to discussions and none of these was initiated by the practitioners. However, the period between January and March 2010 saw 29 responses to discussions and two new discussion threads started by practitioners. By early May, there was increased evidence that the practitioners were beginning to demonstrate greater ownership of the NING and more collaboration using the network, with five postings during the first 2 weeks and two new threads begun by practitioners. March to May also saw the practitioners personalizing their own pages on the NING (changing the colours and fonts, for example) and uploading personal photographs. During the May interviews, practitioners reported that they liked the NING, thought it was useful, and felt that they would continue to communicate with the others in the group if or when the face-to-face group sessions ceased. One stated:

> We all think we're doing our job 'correctly' until you see something else and it's different. It makes you think, and the NING discussions can do that. I'm not really the sort of person who uses 'Facebook' and those kinds of things but it would be good to be able to carry on with the NING if the project ends. I'd probably use it, although time is always an issue.

In the final 2012 evaluations, again there were only very positive comments about the NING:

> I feared using NING at first! Was unsure how to work it. Now I enjoy going on it regularly, like trying to offer advice.
>
> I love the NING. It has a wide variety of information that is specific to my role. The topics discussed are great, as are the links to various articles in Nursery World and other organizations.
>
> I love the NING and go on it every day. I don't always get time to comment but having instant research at your fingertips is a blessing and being able to communicate with other people is very useful. Over the last few months it's like we have been one big baby room, not individual ones.

The feeling of being connected to a large group of people, however tenuously, seemed to increase the practitioners' sense of self-worth in relation to their working practices, both affirming and challenging them but most significantly recognizing their existence.

A second group of project participants comprised 16 local authority advisers. The local authority was extremely keen to join with us in the project and worked hard to both recruit support and to maintain interest, in spite of the weight of its workload and of some of the challenges that caused. The advisory team was mixed and included those with little specialist early years experience or knowledge who had either a general teaching background or special educational needs (SEN) expertise. They were highly challenged by the task of engaging in a case study with settings that knew them in their advisory role – a role that often involved judgements in relation to quality and a duty of care to the children. In this enquiry work they were required to take a rather different approach; they were asked to take on a research perspective, to observe without judgement or mediation. It required them to reflect rather than intervene. They participated in two ways, by taking part in professional development sessions and by undertaking case studies of practice, focusing specifically on observations of talk interactions between individual babies and their carers. Advisors who elected to participate in this project group were supported in developing their case studies, which were drawn from observations made within baby rooms across their region, although excluding those already involved in the Baby Room Project.

While there were clearly tensions for the advisers in undertaking this study – 'This project demanded the team to set aside their "advisory skill set" and observe one baby and capture the communication between the child and its key person' (Harris and Wilson, 2012) – they clearly found involvement in the project supportive of their own professional practice:

> The process of observing without bias, expectation or the ability to make practice suggestions and developments that could impact on children's outcomes was a significant shift in the practice carried out by the advisors. By engaging in the process of case study research, the team were able to observe practice in its 'raw' state. Through the professional development sessions the team's analysis of what they had observed led to rich dialogue, pedagogical reflection and empathy that ultimately will refine and enrich the existing advisory skill set that each individual possesses.
>
> (Harris and Wilson, 2012)

The findings from the responses collected from individual studies were highly significant and included the repeated observation that, although adults were found to talk with babies in devised 'play' contexts, they seemed to miss opportunities for talk during routines such as changing times. The observers found these basic routines to be carried out 'efficiently and hygienically', without unkindness, but talk was only employed to improve the speed of the task. They report that 'the changing of a child is by its very nature intimate and where the adult utilised these times rich examples of early talk were observed as it provided the adult with time to talk with the baby and to respond to their babbling and non-verbal communication'.

It was further identified that the observed practitioners seemed not to understand their role in fostering babies' early talk and creating talk spaces and events, 'although baby rooms are often surrounded by and immersed in talk it was often functional talk between adults. Even though babies can see adults communicating with one another they are not always being communicated with or responded to by the adult'.

It is interesting to see how this kind of systematically collected data and its subsequent analysis is of use in informing the advisers in their professional role and in developing training and support opportunities. Indeed, the local authority advisory team have already indicated how the project will feed into their practice and how it will 'shape the future work of the Quality Team and therefore indirectly impact on the experiential knowledge and aspirations of practitioners working in baby rooms across [the region]'.

The quality of the discussion at the professional development sessions was high and the issues raised, among other things in relation to ethics and involvement, were fascinating. Their rich findings have also contributed to the bank of data collected throughout the project.

Professional development

The project participants have met together for several professional development days. Furthermore, arrangements were made for each participant to visit at least one other represented setting during the course of the project, with a project-funded day set aside for this purpose. Professional development sessions have included a range of activities, such as reference to research, practice, and policy; analysis of the revised proposed EYFS and construction of a joint response to the public consultation for this; critically analysing their own and others' video films of practice; critically reflecting upon aspects of their settings' policies and work with babies; writing, mapping, and debating aspects of their work with babies and their families, and raising issues of concern for discussion.

During the project term, in interviews and in the course of development sessions, the practitioner participants have variously described themselves as being unimportant, invisible and, in one notable, and now much quoted, example, 'the lowest of the low' in relation to other nursery and education employees. We have felt very strongly that this lack of any sense of self-worth or perception of value in their work with babies must invariably impact upon the relationship that practitioners have with their work, the babies and their families. In response to this, a dominant aspect of the development work has been to elevate the status of participants, to ensure they feel that they have a distinct contribution to make – to the babies, parents, and to society in general. This has been achieved in the following ways:

1   We have discussed the fact that families are entrusting the 'most precious thing' in their lives into the hands of relative strangers. In the final evaluation taken of the professional development work and their project involvement generally, and in answer to the question of 'what, if any, difference has your involvement in the project made to your views about your role in the babies' education and care', participants' comments appear to justify this emphasis:

   • 'Makes you think how important our role is as prime carer when parent has left baby in our care.'
   • 'Realization of the importance of your role, how much my input into a child's life can affect them.'
   • 'Being reminded how important our job is with working with babies.'

2   We have been able to establish an Annual Baby Room Conference. This is the only conference that we are aware of that dedicates the entire day's content to the care of babies in formal daycare settings. The core participants have attended each of the first three conferences, alongside academics and advisers. They have displayed elements of their project work in poster presentations and have felt able to discuss their posters with a range of interested visitors. This opportunity has been very well received by the practitioners who, without exception, had never attended a conference or had the opportunity to hear prominent speakers from the field of policy and research, or the chance to debate issues of research, policy, and practice with colleagues practising in the field from across the country.

3   The NING has been emphasized, extended, and maintained. The membership of the NING (the professional online network) has now reached almost a hundred, with members from Scotland to South West England (and one from the USA!). This has provided a safe space for project participants to discuss their concerns, to share successes and worries, and to reach out to colleagues. As already mentioned, they have enjoyed access and links to other sites, including Nursery World and Talk to Your Baby (NLT) and have been provided with policy documents and research information to browse at their leisure. Importantly, this resource has firmly placed the practitioners, who

felt rather neglected and isolated in their practice, very firmly in an extended field of practice with colleagues with whom they feel able to talk. The value of the NING is difficult to overstate.

We remain overawed by the working patterns and conditions of work that baby room practitioners endure. Shifts of work start early and finish late – frequently 7 am to 4 pm – with very few, and very short, breaks. Some practitioners report that they have no break from the baby room, with lunch and tea breaks taken there too. One practitioner reported working from 8 am to 1 pm without a comfort break at all and then a 20-minute break before returning to the baby room at 1.20 pm. These kinds of conditions are not tolerated by society for those working with machinery and yet it is considered safe and appropriate for young women to be in the company of babies, with all their attendant needs, with inappropriate levels of comfort and support themselves. Unfortunately, it seems that market conditions prevail and without any government intervention or investment, this state of affairs will not change. In spite of this, the participants in the Baby Room Project continued to impress us with their energy, their concern to learn, and their generosity in allowing us access to their practice, their aspirations, and their professional lives.

However, what this evidence, from a small sample set, was beginning to demonstrate was a relatively closed or seemingly hidden situation where babies and very young children were being cared for by individuals (predominantly young women) who themselves felt poorly supported and in need of training beyond routine, mandatory, skills-based sessions. During the project, practitioners have described themselves as being unappreciated. Of course, how those working with babies construct themselves and their roles in nursery and in society generally cannot fail to impact on their performance in those roles. Their wellbeing matters to the babies in their care (Elfer and Dearnley, 2007; Rockel, 2009).

Furthermore, our data presented us with further information: the practitioners in baby rooms described their role, and were observed as such in role, as functional – that is, concerned to fulfil the routine requirements of the day, which included feeding babies, cleaning and changing them, putting the babies to bed, and tidying. As a group they are, essentially, pragmatists and defined their work as serving a social need of the moment – that is, 'looking after babies' while their parents worked. In relation to national policy, they are generally the recipients of others' policy information and interpretation, of others' knowledge and understandings, as well as recipients of their instructions in relation to the babies' care, resources, and environments. The practitioners had a limited working knowledge of policy requirements that were delivered 'second-hand', interpreted and abbreviated rather than received by them from a primary source. Overall, there was a helplessness about the participants' situations and, significantly, a voicelessness implicitly required of them.

Professional dialogue

The professional development aspect of the project has deliberately focused upon some key themes: talk, environments, and relationships (which will also be addressed in Chapters 4, 5, and 6). While these three elements clearly overlap, some quite separate issues relate to each. Of these three themes, talk became the central issue in two ways. First, it became clear very early on in the sessions that the practitioners were extremely keen to talk to each other. After the first, somewhat tentative meeting, the practitioners demonstrated how eager they were for contact with others working in the same domain, for a range of reasons; for example, to compare experiences, to share incidents, to compare work patterns, to compete (in terms of quality of care), and to gossip (about their job circumstances). Second, and of paramount importance, we were gathering evidence (from observations, interviews, and research conversations) that talk with babies was not a central feature of baby room life.

Throughout the project, we have been repeatedly told by the participants of the value to them of time to talk to each other. There is ample research relating to the significant effects of dialogic exchange between teaching professionals (see, for example, Medwell et al., 1998) and of the acclaim received for the Reggio Emilia approach to the shared understanding of children and the pedagogy surrounding them (Rinaldi, 2005). It seems that, in spite of research knowledge in relation to the impact of dialogic exchange there remain many employees of nurseries without opportunities to improve their practice and to develop professionally through networks of practice. It seems that baby room practitioners in particular are either not targeted for professional development programmes or find that such programmes are not targeted at baby room practice. Yet it could be argued that they are employed in one of the most responsible positions in daycare. In his work to define and understand the power of thought, Smith (1992) claims that the ability to think 'depends on the company we keep; it depends on the way we perceive ourselves, which depends on the way other people treat us' (p. 125), and this claim has gathered support during the project term, together with the idea of 'learning in companionship' (Whitehead, 2009).

During the project, we noted that the participants were very enthusiastic to talk to each other. The content of their talk was invariably self-set – for example, from the first sessions they were heard to be simply swapping details of routines, i.e. 'We start at 8, what time does your shift go from?' 'Do you provide wipes or do parents have to bring them in?' 'Have you got a separate changing area now?' From the evidence, we have learned that this kind of talk has been valuable to them. As the project developed, the nature of their talk changed and the transformative value of this kind of bespoke professional development became clear. The introductory basic details had been exchanged and then, as the confidence of individuals grew, so too did their interest and competence in reflection, narration, and evaluation of their practice. The participants developed a vocabulary, that is, within professional conversations with us and with each other, they had been busy acquiring a new language, a professional discourse, which began to serve their need to understand their professional role. When asked in their evaluations what they had enjoyed about their involvement in the project, expressions such as 'sharing practice', 'meeting other practitioners', and 'talking with others who understand' were the most frequent responses.

Talk with babies

The expectation that babies should enjoy the benefits of intimacy in one-to-one interactions in order to develop a sense of self, 'emotional referencing' (Trevarthen et al., 2003: 10), and opportunities for expression, seems to be a basic provision. Our evidence indicates that in some baby rooms, some practitioners appeared to be unable to offer these kinds of opportunities. A common assumption is made that young, female, practitioners will intuitively engage in 'maternal' interactions with babies and that the babies will benefit from the communicative and cultural modelling that this offers. That this cannot be assumed is a surprising finding from the project. Reasons for this vary but may include: embarrassment and self-consciousness; a lack of understanding that as babies are unable to talk, they need to be talked to; or simply that practitioners themselves have no model of such practice in their own experience and so remain unaware that it may be a crucial element of practice with babies. The project foregrounded the absolute need for talk to occur and during sessions practitioners' own video material was used to show examples of talk practices and provided us with opportunities to discuss reasons why an adult would choose not to talk to babies, with reference to the work of Liz Attenborough (Talk to your Baby, NLT).

Offering opportunities for people who work in baby rooms to express themselves, to question, assert, challenge, defend, explore, and examine their behaviour, motivations, and practice, created the potential for a professional sense of responsibility to develop and this seemed to be evident in some of their evaluative responses:

> . . . [it's] widened my understanding by making me take a step back and think about some situations.

I now sometimes question what I do, and who it actually benefits.

I have looked around my baby room and tried to see it from a babies [*sic*] view, and made appropriate changes.

Sowing the seeds of opportunity for professional reflection does not necessarily ensure professional growth and development, but it is a sound beginning. The new 'voices' of the practitioners in the project were heard and respected in the development sessions, which seemed to support them in beginning to value their work with babies.

And finally

In the current quest for daycare for babies, demands are being made on young practitioners to invest emotionally in their relationships with babies and their families, which is clearly evidenced in our project story. However, the national picture accompanying this story, although changing rapidly in response to political motivations and priorities as discussed earlier, urgently needs also to demonstrate its willingness to invest in this care, universally for all babies and young children, and to also invest in those employed to work with babies. In the Baby Room Project, it was evident that more consideration needs to be given to the daily lives and wellbeing of babies as well as the daily lives and wellbeing of those employed to care for them.

3 Baby care professionals

What is the big picture of childcare?

In Chapters 1 and 2, some of the debates in relation to childcare have begun to emerge and at this stage there appear to be many questions but few answers. These core questions remain: As a democratic society, what do we want childcare to do for us? And who can be helped and what are the risks? Into this mix, discussion of aims and objectives, decisions about how children can be cared for, as well as who will care, need also to be considered. Services need to be funded, supported, and sustained, as continuity of care provision is helpful to individuals and to communities. And so, while ideally the question of who will provide out-of-home care should be free of economic constraints, affordability is inevitably one of the ingredients. Currently, in New Zealand, questions are being raised about the kind of care for children under 2 years that is in the children's best interests, while acknowledging that the need to work and to care for infants and very young children is a complex issue, and that more support should be given for parental care of those children under 12 months (Carroll-Lind, 2011). In England, however, it seems that current systems are enacted almost by default, with little public, policy or political consideration being given to wide-ranging questions of whether infants should be cared for outside of the home, what 'quality' looks like for the care of infants beyond basic health and safety issues, and whether the best interests of the infant are being served. Indeed, although Pugh (2010: 17) argues that

> parents currently feel torn by the dual messages coming out of government – return to work in order to earn your way out of poverty, on the one hand, but parenting is the most important role that you will play and your child's future depends on the quality of your relationship, on the other hand . . .

many of the arguments for early intervention in children's lives rest on the need for savings to be made by the nation – by mitigating against later care and support needs and calls on the public purse, with the resulting 'instrumentalist view of parents' by the state (Pugh, 2010: 15) and a resulting instrumentalist view of childcare.

Equally, it seems that little attention has traditionally been given to who enacts the caring role for infants in daycare contexts, other than the need for care to be affordable. The result of this neglect appears to be that young women have taken on low-paid care roles if no other occupational or educational route was available. Thus, childcare, which has traditionally demanded few if any academic qualifications, has been driven by assumptions that young women who are also 'low-schooled workers' (Peeters, 2008) are genetically predisposed to take on these roles. This assumption has been politically convenient, as it ensured that the costs of childcare were kept low through the minimum wage responsibilities of employers. This has also been combined with the shift of priorities from state-funded provision to for-profit businesses. The burden of costs then falls on parents, many of whom pay large percentages of their earnings on childcare (see, for example, *The Parent Trap*, Foster, 2012), thereby ensuring that challenging tensions are maintained for working parents. The complexities surrounding this argument, including reference to feminist debates, will be further considered in later chapters. For now it is sufficient to highlight the possibility that there may be a broad range of underlying reasons for not funding investments into childcare and maintaining a fragmented and ill-defined service, including perhaps sustaining traditionalist arguments regarding attachment, inequality in employment opportunities, and consolidation of social stratification.

Who cares?

Who cares for babies and very young children in out-of-home institutions is both contentious and complex. The statutory adult/baby ratio in England of 1:3 is expensive in staff terms and because of the business model employed, the young, inexperienced, and poorly qualified staff in nurseries work with the youngest babies (Goouch and Powell, 2012). The most experienced and qualified staff are employed to work with those children nearest to transition to school. This situation, which seems to prevail in settings in England and elsewhere, presumes a variation in levels of intellectual engagement and support for cognitive development that requires similarly differing levels of qualifications and experience. Additionally, professional development support for baby room practitioners who are in employment is elusive. The reasons for this are also complex but may include:

- Work with babies is frequently believed to consist solely of functional routines, i.e. washing, feeding and resting, and therefore little is required of those who take on this work.
- Professional development is costly. It requires temporary staffing cover as well as the cost of the programme or course.
- Professional development may also be costly in terms of additional, contingent salary demands, i.e. the more qualifications, the higher the remuneration demanded.
- Very few opportunities exist for professional development focused specifically on babies from birth to 2 years.
- Some owners/managers believe that it is disruptive to babies' attachments if practitioners leave their care, however temporarily, to engage in professional development.

It is also reported that, in England, while staff costs account for 77 per cent of the total costs of providers of childcare, in recent times there has been 'upwards pressure on staffing costs because of increases in the qualification levels of those working in the sector', even though 'pay levels in the childcare sector remain below the national average, in spite of these increases' (DfE, 2012: 4). Because of these costs and the fact that childcare providers appear to be struggling to survive economically, Professor Nutbrown presented a *Review of Early Education and Childcare Qualifications* (Nutbrown, 2012b).

The childcare picture in England, but also in other English-speaking countries, is emerging:

- For national and personal economic reasons, women who are mothers are being encouraged by the state, by national governments, to return to, or to begin, employment.
- Childcare, which is now dominated by for-profit businesses, is expensive for parents of infants in particular.
- The women employed to care for infants are inexpensive as they are frequently young, inexperienced, and have few qualifications.
- Mandatory professional development for these employees is focused on functional aspects of health and safety.

This picture appears bleak, and in general terms, for the workforce, it is. Those practitioners who care for infants work very long shifts; have few, short breaks in their day; rarely engage in work-focused dialogue or have opportunities to share work-focused time with colleagues; have low self-esteem and occupy a lowly status in society (Powell and Goouch, 2012). And yet, in general, these young carers manage to cope, perhaps through goodwill and commitment, perhaps because of the unique genetic tendencies humans possess to provide care and comfort to more vulnerable others (Gopnik, 2009), or perhaps because they recognize the rather specialized position they are in. As one baby room practitioner commented, 'they're leaving the most precious thing in the world with us, aren't they?' (practitioner interview). Yet is 'coping' what is demanded of baby room staff by society? Does this constitute 'quality' or are 'regulatory regime[s], the education and support services and the monitoring of practices for under 2-year olds fall[ing] short of what is in their best interests' (Carroll-Lind, 2011: 43), as some fear may be the case in New Zealand? In the international rush to achieve maximum percentage out-of-home care for infants, it may be that 'who cares' for babies is being overlooked, either intentionally for reasons of cost or maintaining the status quo, or simply through ill-informed political expedience.

What's in a name?

New arguments, internationally focused, now centre on job descriptions, which may be a distraction if not a complete red herring, or may be absolutely fundamental to resolving some of the tensions in the role and in how provision is framed in contemporary society. Specifically, the notion of whether childcare constitutes a 'profession' is under review by researchers, commentators, and others. And the term is defined, described, and attributed differently across areas of childcare. The way in which society constructs the nature and embodiment of those employed to work with babies is central to how the young, mostly female employees view themselves and are viewed by others. The descriptor given, in contemporary discourse in England, to people who work in nurseries is 'practitioner'. This rather ambiguous term seems to reflect the ambiguous nature of the role, which is expected, but frequently not defined. It is neither teacher nor caregiver, but merely an employee who practices, although the nature of the practice is hard to conceptualize from this term. Nutbrown's (2012b) *Review of Early Education and Childcare Qualifications* has also sought to gather consensus in relation to how those working in nurseries should be described. How we 'name the world' of course influences how we act upon it, and so perhaps naming the role of employees in nurseries may help to 're-envision' the early childhood worker (Moss, 2006). In turn, some of the tensions that exist, both in the discourse and ultimately the practice, could become transparent, confronted, and challenged. What role(s) are society and parents expecting to be fulfilled in daycare settings? Are baby rooms in daycare simply 'enclosures' as Dahlberg and Moss (2005) describe? And if this is the case, then are baby room employees simply 'minders' until parents resume the 'real' work of parenting?

Professions, professionals, professionalism

Many of those within the early childhood field have raised the question of whether 'professionalizing' early childhood employment will raise the status of the work and the intrinsic worth of early childhood workers. The act of naming early childhood work as a profession simply will not do. In his discussion of the 'four ages of professionalism' in relation to teachers and teaching, Hargreaves identifies two contested notions – of professionalism, described as 'the conduct, demeanour and standards which guide [professionals]', and professionalization, described as the 'status and standing' of teaching (Hargreaves, 2000: 152). Both concepts refer to how teachers are framed, how they are viewed, and how they are represented – that is, their public image. It seems that, in the public domain, the whole notion of what constitutes teachers and teaching has been constructed and reconstructed over time and has been differently dominated by political and other interests throughout the last century or more. Hargreaves' argument is that images of teachers have been changed in relation to teachers' professionalism and professional learning during distinct historic phases, which he defines as a 'pre-professional age', 'the age of the autonomous professional', 'the age of the collegial professional', and 'the fourth age, post professional or post modern'. In the images that Hargreaves creates of teachers and teaching, there are distinct parallels with childcare practitioners. In particular, where Hargreaves (2000) discusses 'a grammar of schooling' (p. 153) and a 'pre-professional age', it is worth transposing some of the arguments into the field of early years care, to identify similarities and to attempt to define where the arguments might lead, in both political and pedagogical terms, in relation to those who work with babies and very young children.

A **grammar of . . . care:** Hargreaves (2000) takes a view that, in the same way that the grammar of language frames how we speak, the grammar of schooling frames how we educate; its origins can be tracked and once part of the established framework, the grammar becomes institutionalized (p. 153), or perhaps it is simply the case that, with more duplicity and with deference to Lewis Carroll, 'what I tell you three times is true'. Similarly, in the early years field, notions of how young children are 'cared for', ratios, structures and systems, the language of 'care', resistance to 'teaching', apprenticeship models of training, attention to 'pre-school' approaches – all have historical, culturally founded, origins in the history of English nursery education. However, in the case of early years education and care, there are competing discourses. Although in the UK provision for very young children in out-of-home contexts is currently managed through apparently integrated systems of care and education, those children under 2 years of age are deemed to require 'childcare' rather than early education (see OECD, 2006). Thus, the discourse becomes that of health and welfare, placing the 'grammar' of this provision firmly in the field of functional support for babies and their families. Additionally, however, the British government has been keen in recent years to capitalize on research across disciplines to argue for early intervention, and as a result childcare, welfare, and early education have all become part of the early years education and care discourse. The political motivations for this, and for interventions in parenting, may include 'normalizing' (Mozere, 2008: 68), social containment, and compliance. Within contemporary early years 'grammars' exists a very powerful developmental discourse enabling the use of the term 'normal' in relation to babies and young children. The overt problem in relation to a 'normalizing' vocabulary is that it assumes that some children occupy a deficit position, or 'a lack' as Mozere suggests; they need to 'acquire "more" (inches, weight etc), which will then help the child to grow more mature, more adult; as if life were just a continuum of fixed and predictable stages, the same for all' (Mozere, 2008: 68).

As well as employing an early interventionist approach to 'fix' deficits and to ensure the development of 'acceptable adults' (Mozere, 2008: 68), childcare is also politically important as part of an economic argument to ensure low costs at later stages of education and social care and importantly to provide 'enclosures' (Dahlberg and Moss, 2005: 25) to ensure that women can work, as well as being 'factories for the production of predetermined outcomes, instrumental, technical and regulatory' (ibid.). The 'grammar' of care for babies and young children is thus contorted to fit political motivations and to identify and contain children within 'normalizing frameworks'.

Thus whoever is employed to enact provision for babies is caught up in the sometimes competing but invariably persistent debate about education and/or care, which is in place as intervention in order to 'fix deficits', to create acceptable young children/adults, as well as to enclose children while their parents work. This is a tall order, with perhaps conflicting priorities, for young employees with little life experience, education or training and with low pay and low status, who are unable to critically contest dominant and regulatory discourses.

A pre-professional 'workforce'

Hargreaves describes this 'age' of professionalism for teachers as a time when teaching was seen as 'managerially demanding but technically simple . . . as unquestioned commonsense . . . learned through practical apprenticeship', carried out by those who 'devoted [their] self to [their] craft, demonstrated loyalty and gained personal reward through service' and who were simply required to carry out 'the directives of their more knowledgeable superiors' (Hargreaves, 2000: 156). While some may argue, as Hargreaves claims, that teaching itself in England is currently reverting to this historical perspective, it is certainly the case that baby room practitioners could be conceived of within this framework. However, in practice the opposite may be found to be true as, in the Baby Room Project, participants expressed their total commitment to their work with babies and commented that they do 'full-on work', and that 'you have to shut your life off – you can't do anything or be anyone else when you are looking after babies, it is all-consuming work'. This 'vocational' view of their employment is however belied by the – mostly – minimum rates of pay and the often harsh conditions of service they experience.

A 'qualified' workforce

While British government initiatives in recent years have focused on improving qualifications, much of this focus to date, and funding, has been on the creation of a graduate-led and managed workforce rather than supporting the development of the core workforce in nurseries. Although enormous responsibility is placed upon those working with babies, it seems that high-quality initial training, in-service support, and continuing professional development has not generally been experienced by practitioners to inform and develop this important work. Indeed, a recent review of the EYFs (Tickell, 2011) recommended the provision of a 'professional, well supported workforce' for the early years of education and care with a strong recommendation to the British government to 'upskill the workforce' through ensuring high standards of new entry qualifications of the equivalent highly respected status of the NNEB (National Nursery Examination Board) qualification. Additionally in this report, there is a recommendation that the quality of the content of existing training and development should be reviewed. Subsequently, the government commissioned a Review of Early Education and Childcare Qualifications, led by Professor Cathy Nutbrown. In her interim report, she claimed that:

> Good qualifications, taught well, ensure that those training to enter the early years workforce, and those already working with babies and young children, can be supported to develop the right blend of theoretical knowledge and practical skills. When these are combined with the commitment and passion evident across the sector we can expect to see better outcomes for children, in the early years phase and in their later life as well.
>
> (Nutbrown, 2012b: 5)

The notion of a 'qualification', however, also requires deconstruction. In countries such as New Zealand, for example, the term 'qualified' refers to those who have graduated through a degree programme. In England, 'qualified' currently refers to a National Vocational Qualification (NVQ), and generally nursery workers are qualified to NVQ Level 2 or Level 3. This qualification can be achieved in 175 days and is part of a range of NVQ qualifications listed alongside, for example, Beauty Therapy, Carpentry, Nail Technician, Hospitality and Catering, and Hairdressing – a range of skill-based, readily assessed, competence-based occupations. These associations and the experience, academic and skill levels required for NVQs have led to the 'hair or care' label in relation to recruitment of young people into the sector. Indeed, concerns have been raised through Professor Nutbrown's consultation that:

> there appears to be a belief that current level 2 and level 3 qualifica-
> tions do not include sufficient time to study the underpinning
> theory for working with children, that they do not demand that
> learners experience a variety of settings before qualifying, that
> they are too broad (looking at the 0–19 age range, rather than, say,
> 0–7 years), and that they lack sufficient detail on child development
> and observation.
>
> (Nutbrown, 2012b: 7)

Although Professor Nutbrown refers to the idea of qualifications being 'taught well', it appears that the content of such training should be examined, as in a list of 'optional units' at Level 2 are areas that many would consider to be essential units for all those hoping to work with young children, including 'organising environments for children plus their families; assessing children's progress; supporting children under three' (NVQ Courses Information Hub, 2012).

The responsibility of working with babies in daycare is considerable and is growing, with new calls to undertake early interventions to ensure later academic success. Yet a 'policy paradox' is evident in some countries, including England – that is, 'low-schooled workers' (Peeters, 2008) are expected to deliver 'quality' outcomes in their practice with babies and very young children. Additionally, in England, there is now a new requirement for a developmental check on 2-year-olds to be taken and reported by 'a young female workforce, often without many qualifications who often end up working with the very youngest children' (Tickell, 2011: 43). There is international research evidence to demonstrate that 'early intervention contributes significantly to putting children from low-income families on the path to development and success in school' (OECD, 2006: 35) but this will require a level of education, training, and support to ensure that interventions are informed, thoughtful, and sensitive, and with the best interests of the baby and their family in mind.

Hargreaves' description of a pre-professional age of teaching that focused on teaching as a 'craft', requiring little or no training, little or no collaboration with outside agencies, and 'simple' in content, relates closely to images of baby room practice. Furthermore, Hargreaves claims that there is a pervasive public perception, among those whose schooling took place in the pre-professional age, that their 'nostalgia-tinted' ideas remain rooted there. Perhaps this is why images of care, with cradles and bonny babies being attended to by young, au-pair-like employees, rather than a more critically engaged affective and educative context, endure in powerful political and policy-making circles. Hargreaves' (2000) demand for 'an entitlement to and education in a rigorous knowledge base that undergirds professionalism' (p. 170) reflects a more acceptable approach to a new way of thinking about the development of those who 'care' for babies and young children. While the early years field is concerned to professionalize practice and Hargreaves is concerned that teaching is being de-professionalized, the Conservative Secretary of State for Education in England, at the time of writing, is attempting to bind all provision, from birth to 19 years, together into one seamless path, serviced by a single professional entity.

> Well I think the time has come (in fact I think it's long overdue) for us to recognise that all those who work with children – from the moment that they're conceived and born, to the moment that they go out into the world of work – make up one fused and united workforce. All of you are teachers. All of you are involved in the business of education.
>
> (Gove, 2011)

This of course raises the question of whether the nature of the workforce at the beginning or the end of this pathway will drive the professionalization argument, or whether an ill-defined 'inbetween-ness', dominated by a prescriptive curriculum content and pedagogy, will be the ultimate outcome. Additionally, the question of who will pay for the values-laden but also highly expensive 'teacher' label has not been considered.

The insiders

Within these debates, which create uncertainties about the social worth of childcare work, the public status of those employed within it, and the lack of stated societal goals for the care of very young children, there remains a body of young women who are ill-supported to develop 'the architecture of professional selves' (Stronach et al., 2002). Neither primary caregiver nor nursery nurse, nor, in spite of the Secretary of State's rhetoric, do they claim to be, seem to wish to be or are trained to be teachers. Rockel describes a somewhat different perspective on those who work in childcare services in New Zealand, although the naming of the role is equally contested there, with 'caregiver', 'educator', and 'key teacher' all presenting challenges. However, in New Zealand, some powerful messages emanate from a range of cultural influences:

> In New Zealand, titles such as 'whaea' and kaiako in a Maori early childhood setting (Kaimahi and Kairangahau 2005), and 'faiaga' in a Samoan early childhood setting (Taouma et al 2003), are used in these culturally specific contexts to reflect the mana (prestige) of a teacher or leader. The role of the teacher in such settings is one where responsibilities are undertaken within collective cultural representation rather than one in which an individual takes sole responsibility. This also indicates the complexity of pedagogy based on philosophical and theoretical understandings which are appropriate in a particular context.
>
> (Rockel, 2009)

This notion of 'collective cultural representation' can only be possible where there has been discussion of what constitutes the vision and aims of the kinds of provision deemed appropriate by society, and visions must be affordable. In England, there appears to be a squeeze on professionals and professionalism, in economic, philosophical, and pragmatic terms. That is, there seems to be a mistrust of some of the motives, discourses, and principles of practice within professions and of talk of the 'cultural re-engineering of public sectors' in order to 'remodel existing relations of power' (Ball, 2008: 47). It is in this context that, rather than introducing a new layer of professionals at the beginning of the educative process, from birth, a de-professionalization from the end point appears to be occurring. In Carr's (2003) consideration of education as professional engagement, he troubles over the extent to which teacher knowledge and expertise are founded within professional deliberation and decision or top-down official prescription. The challenge of claiming the worth of the activity as a profession, in Carr's argument, rests upon the nature of those engaged within it:

> If education – conceived as more than just training or drilling – requires capacities to assist others to grow in wisdom and moral discernment, and such wisdom inevitably involves appreciation of and sensitivity to others as ends in themselves more than means to ends, those charged with the promotion of such wisdom would surely need to possess and exhibit some measure of it themselves.
>
> (Carr, 2003: 43)

While at one end of the continuum an often quoted definition of professionalism is 'a general enhancement of occupational qualifications, working conditions and status' or having 'a specific scientific knowledge base, know-ledge monopoly, [a] long academic education' (Moss, 2006: 38), at the other end rests the argument that 'what is distinctive or definitive of professions is that they are in principle moral practices' (Carr, 2003: 37). Among these philosophical debates, in baby rooms, there exists a group of 'employees' whose functions need closer definition and who require a level of agency, as well as support to develop their wisdom, in order to determine their working identities. The dominant models of nursery workers currently assumed, though neither overtly stated in policy or in practice, are, as Moss describes them, that of 'substitute mother', 'technician' or 'researcher' (with the last referenced by the Reggio Emilia approach) (Moss, 2006: 36). The situations within which many of the participants of the Baby Room Project worked, however, failed to allow the dialogic space, dialogic opportunities or contexts to develop a kind of co-constructing, reflective or pedagogically aware 'worker as researcher', but instead frequently teetered between mother and technician, emotional and functional, without the potential for shared or co-constructed learning and development opportunities to help them to shape a professional 'self' (Goouch and Powell, 2012; Stronach et al., 2002).

Conditions of work, pay structures, career structures, external rewards, appraisals, evaluations, and other discursive opportunities all contribute to the value that any worker attributes to themselves, their self-worth and well being. The claim from one participant in the project that 'we're the lowest of the low' had arisen from a vacuum, from the loneliness born out of neglectful leadership and close support. The project participants did not expect 'professionalism' of themselves because it was not demanded of them – by national or local policy or by their employers. Thus, their relation-ship with their childcare role became functional, albeit with emotional narra-tive layers.

The compromise position that childcare workers find themselves in lies in the tension between new roles in a rapidly shifting policy context and the new emphasis of the need to offer professional performances (Stronach et al., 2002) and a 'preoccupation with satisfying the regulatory gaze' (Osgood, 2010: 130). Inevitably, accompanying this uncertain state, then, is an inability to operate in any intuitively valuable way (Goouch, 2010) with babies and young chil-dren. An emphasis on performance to satisfy outside bodies also prohibits opportunities to engage with any sense of confident agency. The notion of heteronomy (Goodson and Hargreaves, 1996: 207), or subordination to the rule of 'others' as opposed to any sense of autonomy in practice, although seemingly counter-intuitive, when the reality of practice demands individual decision-making with little or no support, and yet, in the project, the rationale for practice was frequently heard to be 'because Ofsted says' or 'that's how they do it here'.

'Professionalism from within' (Osgood, 2010: 130)

Alongside the thorny issue of qualifications in the debate about who cares for babies and young children, is the equally thorny issue of class and power. Rather boldly, Vincent and Braun (2011: 776) claim that it is the 'working class women with a low level of qualifications, receiving a low wage, who constitute the majority of the caring workforce [who are] caught within the grasp of a detailed programme of regulation and improvement designed to ameliorate their deficiencies'. It seems that the feelings of being powerless and voiceless (Goouch and Powell, 2012) may be part of the capital that this group offers, if simple, inexpensive, compliance in a state-controlled technicist model but not state-funded provision is required. In her discussion of 'the case for the critically reflective emotional professional', Osgood (2010) claims that contemporary discourse and policy reforms fail to acknowledge the subjectivities of childcare workers. To emphasize the significance of this, two extracts are given below of how participants in the Baby Room Project described 'A Day in the Life of . . .'. They were asked to participate in this as a completely open activity and to post it on the project's virtual network, at an early stage in the project.

Example 1

7.45 am: Arrive at Nursery, check the staff room notice board for appointments, staff cover, sickness etc. and store personal items away.

7.50 am: Set up baby room: take the bins down in the nappy area, turn on cot room monitor and lights, close curtains, open windows/turn on heating, unlock doors etc.

8.00 am: Set up toys in room on floor and table.

8.10 am: Boil the kettle and leave to cool in jugs, collect the register from the office. Write the nappy sheet and daily information sheets for that day.

8.15 am: [Babies begin their day in the Toddler room] Children arrive, staff receive information from parents, and write it in message book if necessary.

8.30 am: Babies and Toddlers are settled in to the room. Breakfasts are prepared and children are fed/assisted with feeding.

If it is a Tuesday the man comes to test the fire alarm!

Example 2

We open at 7 am and children begin arriving from then on. One member of staff is in at 7 and gets the beakers and bottles ready for the day. Other staff arrive between 7.30 and 8.30. Breakfast time is until 8.30 and we offer Weetabix, Porridge or Cheerios (for older babies), when finished each baby who has eaten is wiped with a flannel and their highchair or the table is cleaned. After breakfast, if we are busy we separate into two rooms, some staff go into the baby room with the babies aged up to 12 months and other staff stay in the main room with the older babies, we rejoin for lunch. All babies have free play time where we provide toys and activities for them until about 10 am. It is then snack time and a member of staff will prepare a snack, for example banana, raisins, apple or satsuma. Milk is given according to the babies' individual daily routines as communicated by parents, as are sleep times. With snack the babies have water in their drinks beakers and afterwards are wiped and 2 members of staff will do nappy changing. After snack we have more play time.

All of the contributions were very similar and demonstrated how the project participants worked frequently up to 50 hours a week (with an average of 37.8 hours) and often with no respite or personal space. It also demonstrates how they conceived their day, that it is made up predominantly of routine, of what they do to (or occasionally with) the babies with no self-reference. However, the heteronomous position the participants describe during the project was consistently overlaid with emotional narratives and during the project term a new discourse began to develop where the narratives of outside prescription, of emotional engagement, and of tentative questioning began to emerge. The challenge remains of how this apparently lowly but highly important work can be understood as requiring an investment of the 'substantial selves' (Nias, 1989: 21) of those employed to care. It may be helpful to return to the idea of 'naming' and employing language to construct meaning for those who work with babies and young children, and perhaps the term 'wise helpers' (Moss, 2001: 132), with all that both wisdom and helping imply, could be effectively employed in the context of baby room practice.

4 Relationships
Pentagrams and hearts

It has been argued that people's ideas about infancy, sometimes influenced by evidence from different kinds of studies, can lead to and be shaped by a wide spectrum of perspectives on policies and practices for babies' care (Blenkin and Kelly, 2000). Despite this diversity and the debates in which practitioners, researchers, and policy-makers have engaged, there seems to be a common and shared agreement that relationships matter for babies. Disagreement arises with regard to how and why they matter, what relationships ought to look or feel like, and whether or not they can or should be 'measured'. In this chapter, we explore what research has suggested about relationships and we will also consider the ways that people's perceptions of their roles in those relationships may impact babies' experiences.

What does research suggest about babies' relationships?

- They are important – for numerous reasons and with disparate impacts on babies and other people (in the present and for the future).
- Because they are thought to be important, research continues to explore relationships. They are explored in different ways and for different purposes – mainly through investigations of the nature of interactions and communication.
- They are sometimes used as a performativity measure and such assessments can be a source of anxiety for practitioners instead of a source of support for their own critical reflection and professional development.
- They depend on and are shaped by multiple, diverse factors, not just the attitudes and behaviours of the people immediately involved in relationship events.

- They need to be nurtured and to be based on interpretive criticality in observations, reflections, and communicative acts.

In 2003, the British Educational Research Association's (BERA) Early Years Special Interest Group (SIG) published a review of research on early years pedagogy, curriculum, and adult roles, training and professionalism (BERA, 2003). Considering the effects of adults on young children's learning (and implying all aspects of development), the authors concluded that it is important to consider research evidence about who looks after children in their first 3 years and with what effects, and about the nature of these adults' roles. Many studies focus on adults' relationships with babies rather than babies' relationships. While this might seem to represent the same story, there is a subtle yet important difference in terms of how babies are positioned in studies – as object or subject, as the recipients of others' attention or as the instigators of interactions.

Colwyn Trevarthen's work has been important for highlighting newborn babies' inclination to be social and subsequent endeavours to make and sustain relationships.

> A six-week-old can remember an expression offered by a person on a previous day and intentionally use it as an imitation to provoke joint experience with a different adult. This 'deferred' imitation apparently seeks to identify and maintain a relationship, and to mark and recall shared experiences.
>
> (Trevarthen et al., 2003: 9)

But babies' drive and determination to be social, which Trevarthen suggests are innate human characteristics, are mediated by the uniqueness of each individual and the responses and resources of the family, community, and environment into which he or she is born.

> There are strong individual differences in the way babies behave right from the start ... Differences such as the baby being particularly sensitive to changes in her environment early on, or being able to sleep through a party going on in the same room – can have a profound impact on the people who are caring for her.
>
> (Murray and Andrews, 2000: 11)

As research and public interest in the nature of interactions beyond the family sphere has increased, attention has turned to explorations of the forms of communication (see, for example, Brooker, 2010; Draper and Wheeler, 2010; Hohmann, 2007; Owen et al., 2000; Rentzou, 2011) and the nature of interactions (see, for example, Dalli et al., 2011; Daniel and Shapiro, 1996;

Elicker and Fortner-Wood, 1995; Howes and Ritchie, 2002; Keyser, 2006; Recchia, 2012; Trevarthen et al., 2003; Whalley and the Penn Green Team, 2001) ECEC settings.

Babies and their baby room carers

Degotardi and Pearson (2009) propose that relationships in ECEC contexts consist of interactions and exchanges in a cycle of reciprocity and continuity that 'draws attention to the subjective, psychological components of a relationship, comprising internal cognitive, motivational, and emotional states' (p. 145)

The Baby Room Project participants provided extensive evidence of the intellectual (cognitive) and emotional demands they perceived their work entailed as well as the physical exertion involved. Discussions regularly ranged around issues such as sore knees and backache, having to contain one's feelings regardless of how difficult this might be, as well as the constant need to be mindful of what the babies were doing, what they might need or want to be doing next and how these could be managed within the established routines for the day. Although they worked closely with many babies over the course of a week, each participant was principally responsible for attending to particular babies and for establishing 'positive relationships' with these babies and their families. This reflected the 'Key Person Approach' that had been adopted in their settings and is advocated in the EYFS as well as in other countries' construal of the basis for relationships. This approach has been described as 'an involvement, an individual and reciprocal commitment between a member of staff and a family. It is an approach which has clear benefits for children and parents, the key person and the nursery' (Elfer et al., 2003). The theoretical underpinnings stem from attachment theory (Bowlby, 1969) originally based on studies of (western) infants and their mothers (including Ainsworth et al., 1978; Stern, 1977). The central argument is that,

> secure adult–child attachments form the basis for children's psychological well-being. Infants are assumed to have innate attachment behaviours such as clinging, crying, and smiling, which, when activated by the presence of the attachment figure, elicit adult behaviours that provide them with the security and emotional warmth they need to thrive.
>
> (Degotardi and Pearson, 2009: 145)

Attachment theory has had a significant and substantial effect on beliefs and practices concerning babies' social and emotional connections but,

> There is no support for the claim that an infant or toddler must be
> cared for by the mother to develop well emotionally and cognitively,
> but normally a mother will have strong motivation to be the child's
> closest companion, with support from the father who shares affec-
> tion for the child.
>
> (Trevarthen et al., 2003: 130)

By reconceptualizing babies' interactions, Degotardi and Pearson acknowledged the wide network of attachments that babies can form with other
people. Judy Dunn (1983, 1988, 1993) has contributed significantly to this
field, demonstrating the complexities of young children's relationships
with, among others, their friends, siblings, peers, and children of other ages
(see, for example, Kernan and Singer, 2011; Woodhead et al., 1998). Concerning
the enduring effects of babies' and young children's relationships, David
(2009: 88) has proposed that, 'pleasurable interactions during the first two
years provide the scripts which children adopt in their later friendships'.

Despite these findings, dyadic relationships continue to be constructed as
the centrepiece of babies' social explorations. A key message from any dyadic
attachment theory-based research would therefore seem to be that a principal
purpose of this special relationship with a baby should be to provide a platform
from which they will feel confident to instigate and sustain positive relationships with other people and the opportunities that these then afford in many
contexts and circumstances.

The mother–child dyad as a model for considering and comparing babies'
relationships with other people retains an enduring impact. The warmth, intimacy, attunement, and responsiveness attributed to positive maternal care are
assumed to be at the core of babies' positive relationships with other carers (see
Elfer, 2006). These relationships are framed principally from a developmental
perspective and seek to provide a firm foundation from which a baby can
develop emotionally and socially. Mary McMullen and her colleagues in
Indiana (McMullen et al., 2009: 22) have explored babies' pro-social behaviours from this basis and state that all babies 'have their own personal characteristics and preferences, temperaments and needs (Field, 2007), and they need
to feel that their caregivers value and respect those traits (Abbott and Langston,
2005)'. Similarly, Recchia has observed that different developmental patterns
affect how relationships develop and says that these have consequences for
babies' sense of security and the closeness that is established with a carer. But
she asserts that despite the individual differences,

> Child development experts agree that best practice in infant and
> toddler care-giving requires a strong focus on building positive and
> trusting relationships, and that this relationship-focused care-giving
> should have as its goal the development of secure attachments

between children and their caregivers (Raikes 1996; Howes and Ritchie 2002).

(Recchia, 2012: 1)

The focus of studies about relationships is not narrowly confined to cognitive or behavioural domains of development (although domains are sometimes isolated in research); nor are they based on assumptions that infants are unresponsive or lack agency. Rather, these studies assume that development is multi-dimensional, may be observed as multi-sensory and, by including the social and cultural, also imply a moral dimension (Blenkin and Kelly, 2000).

From these theoretical positions, the baby is both the start and end points for the focus of empirical attention. But studies of mother–infant dyads have also highlighted how a mother's emotional and mental health (Martins and Gaffan, 2000; Teti et al., 1995) and material and social circumstances (for an ecological design, see Reifsnider et al., 2005) contribute to her ability to form a positive, warm, strong, and secure attachment.

Carers' wellbeing

The other girls don't want to work in the baby room. They can't hack it because of the noise, all the crying. (Ella)
If you can't stand the heat, get out of the kitchen. (Sophie)
Sometimes they all start, one sets them all off. That's really hard and you can see some of the girls need a break and you need to be able to say to them, 'go and have five minutes, have a cup of tea' but you can't because of ratios . . . this woman who used to work with me kept going to the toilet. She didn't need the toilet; she just needed to escape for a few minutes' peace. (Ella)
People like that shouldn't work in the baby room; you have to be able to handle the pressure. (Sophie)

(Development session dialogue, September 2011)

Attachment theory has been challenged as conceptually constraining, neglecting the contribution of professional theories to the forming of relationships, and dyad-centric (Degotardi and Pearson, 2009). Nevertheless, while it persists as the dominant theoretical foundation for the establishment of babies' relationships in daycare settings, we should ask questions (1) about why this might be and (2) consider the implications about the emotional and mental health of all those involved. Comparatively speaking, little attention has been given to the wellbeing of babies' carers in formal settings or to the consequences of their emotional or psychological states, although there have been some studies within this terrain (see, for example, Calder, 1994; Elfer, 2006, 2012; Goldschmied and Jackson, 1994; Hopkins, 1988).

If the theoretical basis for establishing secure attachments is transferred from mother–baby to other carer–baby dyads or groups (where an adult may be responsible for three babies simultaneously), it seems sensible if not vital to consider these other carers' welfare too. Sophie's contention that 'people like that' (implying they lack emotional resilience) should not be employed to care for babies is debatable; but that conditions exist in which practitioners feel little or no escape from unremitting emotional and physical pressures, while being responsible for the welfare of the youngest children, is inexcusable.

The emotional demands of caring for young children have been emphasized by Colley (2006) and Osgood (2012). In a study of the dispositions that early years practitioners in the USA felt were vital for their roles, Colker identified twelve traits, including passion, perseverance, patience, pragmatism, and a sense of humour (Colker, 2008). Although Colker's study was concerned with dispositions that are suitable for the general breadth of ECEC work, the 43 interviewees' responses could provide insights into the qualities deemed necessary to deal with the stresses inherent in the role. In her analysis of emotional capital, Colley has argued that employers exploit young women's emotional labours in caring roles. Of course, this is likely to apply to a small number of men in this role too.

> In occupations like childcare and care of the elderly, the management of one's own and others' feelings is not a private adjunct to work, nor a sub-category of caring. It is a key feature of the workplace, a form of paid labour, or to be more accurate, of labour power – the capacity to labour, which can be ever more exploited by those who own the means of production for private profit.
>
> (Colley, 2006: 25)

In this way, accountability for emotional labour becomes the shared responsibility of a society or the community rather than the individual alone. This strengthens the case for concerns about what is expected of babies' carers, why and how they (learn to) cope with such demands or do not.

The work of Elfer and Manning-Morton in England has been important for highlighting the need for support to help deconstruct emotional practice (e.g. Elfer, 2012; Elfer and Dearnley, 2007; Manning-Morton, 2006). This is common to other forms of emotional work (social work, nursing) but does not appear to have been widely recognized or implemented in ECEC and certainly not in daycare for babies.

In New Zealand, Rockel and Craw (2011) have argued that dialogue concerned with infant–toddler pedagogy must incorporate considerations of the infants' (un)happiness and the goals and values of parents and babies' carers. In our own interviews with parents in England, a discourse of happiness was evident too.

> It's on my way to work and I chose them [the setting] because the room was full of natural light and I thought that Katie would be happy there.
>
> (Interview with Andrea, mother of Katie, 13 months, July 2011)

Rockel and Craw refer to workplace wellbeing and the distress that two teachers experienced, but this was not the focus of their study, which concerned the babies' happiness. They state:

> In relation to early childhood pedagogy, the notion of (un)happiness involves complex desires by teacher, parent and child for an ethic of care in the 'here and now'. To clarify understandings of (un)happiness discourses, and their effects, the conversations that relate to the value-base for each person need to take place.
>
> (Rockel and Craw, 2011: 127)

It is our contention that this is equally valid for considerations of practitioners' (un)happiness, which may inform reflections about the babies' well being. Trevarthen and his colleagues refer to the 'emotional climate of the establishment'. In so doing, they imply attention to the general sense of wellbeing among the staff team as well as that of the babies and young children in their care (Trevarthen et al., 2003: 30).

Love and emotional dependency

Happiness, secure attachments, intimacy, warmth, responsiveness, companionship, passion, and affection are qualities associated with the relationship between babies and their carers. The concept of 'love' is less often applied and is most commonly referenced in work about babies' relationships within the context of their families: Bowlby (1965) and Trevarthen et al. (2003) about mothers in particular, as well as families more generally and by implication 'care communities'; Dunn and Kendrick (1982) about siblings; Smith (2006), Chambless and Jack (2007), and Rice et al. (2010) about grandparents; Roberts (2010: 56) about companions – parents, other adults, and children who see them regularly and know them well; Gerhardt (2004) predominantly about parents; Robinson (2003, 2008), Vincent and Ball (2001), Goldshmied and Jackson (2004), and Biddulph (2010) about parents and professionals who work with babies and/or very young children; and Page (Nutbrown and Page, 2008;

Page, 2011) uniquely and specifically about professionals. In general, a gendered construct of early childhood care as maternal or feminized seems to have led to a deficit of studies exploring the concept of love in babies' relationships with fathers or with male childcare professionals, although studies do include or focus on male carers as attachment figures, but without reference to love (e.g. Cameron, 2006; Cameron et al., 1999; Waller, 2009). The alternative seems to be the psychoanalytic literature of the incorrectly named 'Elektra Complex', which concerns psychosexual desire of girls aged 3 and older for their fathers' love (a misnoma because there is no evidence in Greek mythology that Elektra, the daughter of the King of Mycenae, Agamemnon, was sexually motivated).

Nutbrown and Page (2008) have argued for an honest and open discussion in the sector, to include representatives from government, of 'professional love'. Page has explored the idea in depth and asked whether mothers want professional carers to love their babies and how considerations of love may influence mothers' decisions about employment after childbirth. Professional love is described as complementary to parental love for a baby, and 'the intellectual experience of *pedagogical loving* requires motivational displacement and involves developing deep, sustaining, respectful and reciprocal relationships' (Page, 2011: 313). The issue of reciprocity seems to be at the nub of issues of insecurity: while the mothers in Page's study indicated that they wanted carers to love their babies (even if they did not use the word love), there was also an underlying tension for one mother in particular. Page suggests that discussions between practitioners and babies have failed to explore beliefs about love and loving relationships and she calls for attention to this gap. But her work also suggests that research could usefully explore not only the question, 'do mothers want professional carers to love their babies?', but also, 'do mothers want their babies to love professional carers?'

Lynch (2007) has proposed that the kind of primary care that represents love in professional caring relationships must be developed and nurtured over time. As such, she effectively argues that love cannot be bought in bite-size chunks of care. Vincent and Ball (2001) and Biddulph (2010) agree with this perspective and what has been called the commodification of love. Certainly, if love depends on nurtured reciprocal interactions, then time would appear to be an important ingredient for loving relationships to be developed. Studies of continuity of and in care (e.g. Lash and McMullen, 2008; Noddings, 1984; Recchia, 2012) confirm the importance of opportunities to develop enduring relationships, including those that withstand transitions (such as from the baby room to the toddler room). In such cases, the relational processes are supported and constrained by environmental factors and structures. The project participants explored their inabilities to sustain relationships with babies once they moved on to another part of the setting and some expressed a sense of their own loss, while we also witnessed examples of toddlers' demonstrations of their loss at moving on.

> While Sophie was giving me a tour of the nursery we came across a little girl, a toddler, in one of the rooms. When she saw Sophie she lifted her arms up to her straight away and beamed. Sophie explained that she'd had a very close relationship with this child when she'd been in the baby room. She seemed pleased that this girl had demonstrated her affection in front of me as though it was a sign of her ability to form strong and lasting bonds with the babies. In fact I wasn't sure who was more pleased. When we left the toddler room, the little girl screamed in distress as Sophie guided me to another part of the setting.
>
> (Field notes following nursery visit, November 2009)

The making and severing of bonds is a difficult business. The participants in the project argued repeatedly that good relationships with babies relied on the emotional stability of baby room staff.

> What you don't want is people, the kind that only want to be in the baby room because they have issues, the sort who need to be loved and they think they can get that from the babies. They get that more unconditional kind of love they don't get from the older children who are more independent. They're emotionally needy.
>
> (Carla, development session, May 2011)

> Sometimes we've had girls, well usually it's older women actually, who come and want to work with the babies because they have a need to be loved themselves. This isn't good for the babies.
>
> (Lena, manager interview, June 2010)

Emotional neediness is a complex issue but these examples from the project of a general rejection of this (perceived) characteristic as being unsuitable for work with the babies arguably strengthens our call for greater attention to carers' emotional health and wellbeing. This has implications for policymakers and providers/managers, for as Elfer and Dearnley (2007: 278) have argued,

> It needs to be recognised that resources have to be allocated for the time and facilitation for staff to think about and process the individual feelings evoked by their emotional work with the children. This involves an attitudinal shift too, seeing reflective practice as an entitlement of staff, both legitimate and necessary, if changes in professional practice are to be facilitated and sustained.

In addition to considering the knowledge, experience, and skills of practitioners and their 'espoused theories, beliefs, values and assumptions' (Rockel and Craw, 2011: 122), more work may be needed to explore dispositions. Critical research may help to reveal taken-for-granted discourses about the characteristics deemed (by policy-makers, childcare providers, practitioners, and parents) to be important for work with babies, and observation and dialogue with babies' carers may help us to infer what babies themselves might value in different contexts and activities.

A tick-box culture?

Since the US National Institute of Child Health and Human Development (NIHCD) conjectured that the quality of interactions is a cornerstone of good practice to support babies' development (see, for example, NIHCD 1998, 2000, 2001), there have been many attempts to create criteria by which the 'goodness' of quality can be measured. These include measurement instruments such as the Arnett Caregiver Interaction Scale (Arnett, 1989) and Wellbeing and Involvement Scales (Laevers, 1997).

Although such scales have been widely employed in many different cultural contexts, the identification and assessment of interactions as constituting good or poor relationship experiences is highly problematic (Carl, 2007). Through our professional network, we have been particularly concerned to hear anxieties about the ways in which scales have sometimes been hijacked and employed as an instrument of summative assessment, for the creation of hierarchical grades or league tables of performance, rather than a tool for critical and formative professional dialogue and practice development. But the more such tools and other prompts for critical professional reflection are taken in-house by practitioners, the less they become the preserve of governments and other figures of authority as means of subjugation and control, or experienced as such.

Constructs of what represents good (or bad) quality relationships will be culturally specific, will vary, and will tend to reflect what is observable and what the observer notices, rather than babies' subjective experiences. When relationships are deconstructed, the key constituent elements are identified, broadly speaking, as the dynamics of interactions (usually dyadic or tryadic) and the forms and functions of communication. How does a baby construct a good quality interaction? Some attempts have been made to define quality from a young child's perspective (see review by Mooney and Blackburn, 2003). But these studies have sometimes been designed within the frame of an adult's perspective and agenda, translate the specific into a universal construct – (all) children's views of quality – and do not include babies and children under 2 years (although Danko-McGhee, 2011, employed an innovative approach to study aesthetic responses to art involving babies as young as 3 months and head-cams are increasingly being employed to gain a baby's-eye view of the 'objective' world). This does not mean that such studies cannot provide useful and important findings for consideration and critical reflection but should raise a concern where they are imposed as the only – or the only formal – means by which a baby's relationships are contemplated to inform practice. Nor does it mean that the difficulties associated with unpacking interactions and how these may have been experienced by a baby should discourage pro-active and ongoing attempts to deconstruct relationships by examining inter-actions and communicative events and thinking about their effects on all involved.

Reconstructing interactions

From research in Australia, Degotardi has suggested that these reflections should start with observing interactions in the setting (which may be retro-spective using filmed observations). She found that when practitioners were asked to think about their interactions with infants, there were qualitative differences in the participants' interpretive complexity. Grouping by complexity then revealed correlations with the kinds of experiences that were offered to the babies and, perhaps more importantly, were associated with whether or not the infants' point of view was integral to the activity of reflecting:

> Low-complex interpretations were brief, limited in detail and largely described observable, physical behaviour. More complex interpreta-tions included a rich diversity of interpretive ideas which demon-strated an understanding of the infant's subjective point of view, as well as interconnections between the infant's behaviour, her/his psychological states and features of the social world.
>
> (Degotardi, 2010: 28–9)

What's going on?

Degotardi also emphasizes the effect that different kinds of activities can have on the interactions themselves and on practitioners' reflections on these events. She suggests that routine activities involve less complex interactions and fewer interpretive comments from practitioners (taking the babies' perspectives into account). This finding was confirmed in our own research: the participants' 'Day in the Life' accounts were chronological statements of routine events that happened in the baby room with little qualification or reflection. In contrast, their discussions about the video observations, which involved both routine and spontaneous activities, were more deeply reflective, critical, and involved attempts to take a 'baby's-eye view' of events. An obvious further factor influencing the extent to which interpretation does and does not occur here is the role that a professional development opportunity may play in encouraging and supporting more complex reflection about interaction.

The local authority advisers' case studies for the Baby Room Project also drew similar conclusions from close observations of talk in the baby rooms they recruited for their exploratory research:

> Whilst adults engaged in early talk with the babies in *play* contexts the research team observed that opportunities for talk during *routines* were regularly missed or not fully utilised. For example, 'Changing time: one adult took on the role of changing all the children. This was done efficiently and hygienically and each child was treated the same. There was no unkindness but any talk was just to make the process run smoothly and quickly'. This raised interesting reflections for the research team. As experienced practitioners we recognise the opportunities that routines offer and seek to utilise the rhythms of a baby's day. Discussions have led the team to consider if all practitioners have an understanding of how routine opportunities can provide the practitioner with time to talk with the babies, particularly on a one to one basis. The changing of a child, for example, is by its very nature intimate and where the adult utilised these times rich examples of early talk were observed as it provided the adult with time to talk with the baby and to respond to their babbling and non-verbal communication.
>
> (Harris and Wilson, 2012: 1; emphasis added).

Inside out and outside in

The relationship between a baby's different contexts (or microsystems) has been highlighted as an important feature of how he or she experiences interactions in each context and how they impact on each other (as a mesosystem). What happens in the home is thought to be more influential than what happens in a childcare setting in terms of a baby's development and wellbeing. But some scholars have also explored how perceptions of a person's (particularly a practitioner's) status, role, and responsibilities influence the nature of interactions. Hohmann (2007) has illustrated how parents' expectations and preferences of childcare influence the parent–carer relationship and have an impact on the child (and other children) involved because conflict can arise, in this case concerning the childminder role in England and Tagesmütter role in Germany. Such expectations appeared to be founded on two key factors:

- 'who is seen as competent or in the rightful position to decide on childcare questions [which] may vary according to the issues concerned, and they may change over time' (Hohmann, 2007: 38) and
- 'a relative shortage of childcare provision [which] gives childminders more power to enforce parents' compliance with the childminder's ideas' (Hohmann, 2007: 41).

Hohmann's concept of a 'triangle of care' involving parents, carers, and children was subsequently employed by Brooker to theorize tensions in similar relationships but involving staff from London nurseries, rather than home-based childminders and Tagesmütter. Brooker (2010) noted how 'the differentials of power and expertise . . . may set the parameters for each partner's role, agency and identity within the relationship' (p. 184).

These differentials extended way beyond the immediate childcare issues in question, such as whether a baby should 'self soothe' (see Chapter 8), to influential discourses associated with the status afforded to different social classes and cultures. Where discourses position parents as 'experts', there is a danger of de-professionalizing and lowering the professional esteem of carers by default. In their study of the effects of early education on home learning environments, Hunt and colleagues found that,

> the majority of parents maintain the same level of early home learning once their child starts in a funded childcare place, but that parents in families where adults are not in employment actually do *less* early home learning once their child starts in a funded childcare place.
>
> (Hunt et al., 2011: 9; original emphasis)

Although reasons for the decrease in home learning activity were cited as parents being too busy or the child being increasingly independent, it was also reported that some parents delegated the responsibility for early learning to the nursery and did not see it as part of their own role. In this study, the children were aged 2–3 years and the focus was on learning. The findings might well have been different if the children had been younger than 2 years old and the goals had not been framed within an education paradigm. Vincent and Ball (2006) considered the role that social class might play in attitudes and responses to childcare. Stefansen and Skogen's (2010) research has indicated that social class, in the Norwegian context, may influence ideas about the nature and role of childcare and engagement that is deemed necessary between parents and their children's carers. These examples are connected to Brooker's (2010) contention that attitudes or expectations, which are based on assumptions about class and culture, will influence the nature of relationships as well as the ideas about what a parent's role and a practitioner's role is in the context of a baby's early care or education. The tensions seem often to arise from conflicts about particular ways of caring for a baby in the context of the wider repercussions for practitioners, for parents, and for other babies in the setting: whether or not a baby should be 'allowed' to sleep in the afternoon; whether baby-led weaning is a good idea or not; whether a mother should or should not be permitted to visit the baby room and breastfeed her baby during the day. Respect for diversity as a guiding principle of education and care for babies and young children, combined with critical appraisal of the assumptions that underpin particular ways of caring, can help to reveal hegemonic, discriminatory, and socially and culturally insensitive beliefs and practices (see Browne, 2004, Chang et al., 2000; Robinson and Jones Díaz, 2006; Siraj-Blatchford and Clarke, 2000; Swadener and Lubeck, 1995; Taguchi, 2010a).

While childcare remains largely the preserve of middle-class parents (Vincent and Ball, 2006) who can afford to pay the high costs involved, and while childcare work continues to be seen to be the preserve of poorly paid, poorly educated, and unskilled working-class girls simply doing what comes naturally to females (Vincent and Braun, 2011; and as criticized by Osgood, 2005, 2012), the likelihood is that baby room practitioners will continue to experience tensions in relationships with parents who assume positions of power and attitudes of being more knowing and knowledgeable about what their babies 'need' while they are absent, even though the relationship is different and the context is different. Elsewhere, we have argued that the power differentials have a significant impact on baby room practitioners' perceptions of their abilities to make independent and informed decisions about 'babies' best interests'. Parents are constructed as the most proximal influence and 'policy' is a more distal and ephemeral but nonetheless influential factor (Powell and Goouch, 2012).

Triangles, pentagrams, and hearts

> Over the past 10 years, a groundswell of new empirical studies of triadic and family group dynamics during infancy have substantiated that which family theory has contended for decades: looking beyond mother–infant or father–infant dyads reveals a myriad of critically important socialization influences and dynamics that are missed altogether when relying on informant reports or dyad-based interactions.
> (McHale, 2007: 370)

An holistic, ecological view that attempts to consider the origins of issues or conflict, the perspectives of all involved (including what the parents and practitioners believe about the baby's perspective), what has influenced their beliefs, the power dynamics, the nature of the activity and the impact on all concerned may help to resolve tensions and bring about positive solutions.

The conceptualization of a practitioner's role in relationships with parents and with babies is shaped by wider discourses about the aims and purposes of daycare (or early education) and each parent's own motivations, beliefs, and values. During one of our development sessions for the project, we asked the participants to think about the 'triangle of care' and to reconstruct this in their own terms based on their own experiences of relationships. Their responses supported Brooker's assertion that power differentials are important considerations in relationships between parents and practitioners, as did other evidence we gathered throughout the project. But the most striking and obvious outcome of this exercise was that the participants were adamant that a triangle was not appropriate; that all their relationships were dependent on a much more extensive web of interactions with many different people. Consequently, they theorized their relationships differently by drawing them as intersecting lines in pentagrams and other complex shapes. They represented their relationships as:

- interconnected (particularly in terms of the impact on babies)
- ecological (many different systems with multi-directional effects)
- varying in how positive they felt for the practitioners themselves (shaped and experienced subjectively)
- highly specific – entirely different for each baby they knew and cared for, insisting that it was impossible to draw a picture that represented every baby and each one needed her or his own diagram
- different at different times because of the evolving nature of the relationships and the people who came into and went out of the frame (such as a social worker, a new colleague, an early years adviser, Ofsted inspector, grandparent, childminder or a new sibling for the baby)
- dynamic and dependent on the ways that the practitioner was positioned (personally or professionally) by the other person(s) involved.

These participants suggested to us that when conflict arises, the ripples into and out of the immediate relationship can extend far beyond the triad of parent–child–practitioner and the power differentials, assumptions (or baggage), and behaviours that they bring to the situation. Attempts to forge relationships are supported and constrained by many more factors than those that can be represented by this triad and with reference to the assumptions of class and culture. Although the triad (or a similar one involving another primary carer) was central to participants' theories about the impact of relationships on babies' experiences and their own identities in practice, it was clear that it constituted one part of a highly complicated system in which there was regularly change. It seemed that the dyadic relationship between a practitioner and a baby and the triadic relationship that included a parent was just a small part of a much bigger jigsaw puzzle. Furthermore, the picture in this puzzle did not remain fixed, nor did the number or dimensions of the pieces or the shape of the frame within which it might sit. In Chapter 8, we discuss the value in adopting a critical ecological framework for reflecting on babies' experiences.

Good communication has been identified as central to positively attuned relationships – and the project participants considered the forms of communication that are employed for initiating, sustaining, and repairing them. Although they identified a range of strategies, talk was a key component and it is this specific issue that we will consider in the next chapter.

5 Understanding Talk

We speak it, we read it, we write it; we shout it, we murmur it; we sing it, we pray it, we worry it; we study it, we interpret it; and we think it and think it and think it. We have language on our lips or in our heads from when we get up in the morning until we go to bed at night, and then we dream it.

(Frayne, 2006: 273)

In the beginning . . .

Even before consideration of the importance of talk, the importance of language to our 'human-ness' needs to be stated. Language has often been said to be the essence of what makes us human, what makes us different from other primates. In this chapter, the beginnings of language will first be explored to underpin the significance of talk to babies in the early stages of their lived experiences. In the context of thinking about daycare for babies, the complex web of talk domains (e.g. talk with babies, about babies, as a tool for information cascades), while intrinsically linked, needs also to be examined. Both the context and the nature of talk in baby rooms will be identified and examples drawn from the project data. While recognition, of course, needs to be given to the notion that talk is only one tool in a range of communication strategies, its position as a central aspect of human behaviour must be acknowledged and indeed celebrated.

It has long been recognized that babies tune in to the sounds and patterns of their mother's language before birth (Blakemore and Frith, 2005; Gopnik et al., 1999) and that a baby's brain develops knowledge of language long before 'talk' begins. Research has demonstrated that 'the fetal brain is already becoming attuned to dimensions of speech' (Karmiloff and Karmiloff-Smith, 2001: 44). We seem to be born with an innate preference for distinguishing and tuning into the sounds of language, among the cacophony of other sounds that greet us when we first meet the world (Blakemore and Frith, 2005). Indeed, newborn babies are said to be particularly responsive to the 'emotional tone' (Waxman, 2002: 103) evident in the speech around them, including the 'motherese' often referred to. And, among this new world of first-hand sounds, babies are able to single out the most familiar, the sound of their mother's voice. In these early days and weeks of their lives, babies are said to be developing 'prototypes' of language from which they compare other sounds that they are receiving. It seems that babies store the sound representations that they hear and which influence the sounds they eventually construct themselves, and it is this that ensures that babies' speech is imitative of the sounds of speech around them, sounds that are culturally bound. This prototype then acts as a filter through which sounds that are familiar are caught and re-worked (Gopnik et al., 1999). The work of Patricia Kuhl over many years has taught us how important it is for very young babies to hear talk and to experience 'sound articulation' them-selves (see, for example, Kuhl and Meltzoff, 1996). In their work involving careful analysis of the speech sounds uttered by babies in response to adult voices, Kuhl and Meltzoff have found that hearing speech sounds as well as seeing the adult's moving face provokes babies to produce sounds themselves. Importantly, Kuhl and Meltzoff found that to develop speech, babies need both to hear others' talk and hear the sounds of their own speech efforts to learn to speak successfully. Thus, through experience and experimentation, babies develop their own culturally specific speech. Kuhl and Meltzoff have noted that infant 'cooing' begins at about 4 weeks of age and that by 12 weeks they are beginning to develop the ability to make and shape sounds, with 'speech devel-opment rapidly influenced by experience, especially that gained by infants' own cooing and sound play' (Kuhl and Meltzoff, 1996: 2436). The importance of both hearing and making sounds is emphasized in Kuhl's work and Weir's (1962) seminal study of the ways in which babies re-rehearse sounds and engage in sound play in their sleep monologues further evidences this aspect of very early learning. So, when babies are making sounds that appear arbitrary or random, it may be that they are creating a 'mouth to sound map' (Gopnik et al., 1999: 124) that will form a platform from which later word learning will develop. Greenfield describes this as a 'framework of reference, an increasing degree of meaning to ongoing experience' (Greenfield, 2000: 52). The vital importance of early experiences of close interaction has been explored by researchers (see, for example, Gopnik et al., 1999; Trevarthen, 1998; Trevarthen and Aitken, 2001) by closely observing the ways in which intimate 'conversa-tions' between babies and significant adults are often led by the baby and rewarded and sustained by warm responses and turn-taking:

> Even in the first weeks of life, interaction between parents and infants assumes, with vocalisations or simple gestures, the turn taking and reciprocity of later linguistic exchanges. Within this nurturing

> communicative context, infants learn to initiate and lead interaction. Later as cooing turns to babbling and then to first words, infants begin to accumulate knowledge about how to answer different types of speech acts.
>
> (Karmiloff and Karmiloff-Smith, 2001: 150)

What we learn from this research evidence is that before birth, immediately after birth, and in the first weeks of life, a baby's brain has been 'actively processing the language in their environment' (Karmiloff and Karmiloff-Smith, 2001: 54) from a variety of stimuli including the tones, patterns, and structures of language. It is from this early brilliance, in relation to mapping speech sounds and tunes into the range of interactive experiences, that babies are able to launch into the symbolic world of meaning-making, according to the families, communities, and cultures in which they are immersed.

'The living union of sound and meaning that we call the word' (Vygotsky, 1986: 5)

Language learning is pivotal in ensuring learning of all kinds and Vygotsky's claim that 'the child's intellectual growth is contingent on his mastering the social means of thought, that is language' (Vygotsky, 1986: 94) is borne out by our experience of living with and working with babies and young children. The symbolic nature of language is understood as very young children are introduced to the names that make up the experienced world. Words, or attempts at words, begin to stand for something important in babies' lives. Language as a tool to achieve functional ends as well as for ensuring action and interaction is learned, as babies are sensitive to the attuned responsiveness of mothers. Through playful interactions, which have been called 'photoconversations' (see, for example, Trevarthen and Aitken, 2001), babies are able to engage in 'mutuality in action' (Bruner, 1986: 59), that is the kind of dialogue that involves sound, action, and warmth of engagement. Bruner talks of the dual focus of speech acts; that is, both the 'locution' – of what is actually said – as well as the illocutionary force – indicating what is intended (Bruner, 1986: 65). Thus, the word 'cup' could be uttered as a naming activity or further as demand. And so, not only are babies engaging in 'word-to-world mappings' (Waxman, 2002: 104) but also beginning to grasp 'the symbolic and referential power of words' (ibid., p. 107), which leads them to employ language in a range of extended contexts. Indeed, Waxman claims that word-learning stands at the very intersection of language and cognition, and serves as the gateway to subsequent development in both domains' (ibid., p. 103).

If, as Bruner (1986) claims, 'Language is our principal means of referring' (p. 63), then early shared engagements, early dialogue, the first speech acts in which babies take part contribute to their stored language, the vocabulary and so 'the system of language [is acquired] from his speech community' (Volosinov, 1973: 53). The acquisition of language does not occur in a vacuum but rather in the company of interested 'others', primarily in the first instance, the mother, family, and principal caregivers. Language, of course, does not consist only of vocabulary but of meanings and these occur naturally through 'conversations' with adults (Vygotsky, 1986). Thus we learn that for babies to learn language, to communicate and to express themselves, there is an essential requirement of 'an interplay between factors inherent in the child and factors within the environment' (Waxman, 2002: 125), an environment that will include the input and interactions as well as the 'ambient language' (Kuhl and Meltzoff, 1996) that surrounds babies in their early lives. There is no intention here to suggest any formulaic approach to the support of babies' language learning. Rather, it is suggested that it is from an often haphazard language environment that babies draw their language information, although there may be obvious impacts from over-crowded home environments, other background stimuli such as televisions, and limited joint attention episodes (David et al., 2003). However, with the knowledge that 'brain cells will proliferate at the rate of 250,000 per minute' and that very young babies from birth are exploiting and processing experiences, it is reassuring that it is not 'material wherewithal' that matters to this remarkable brain growth but that 'stimulation is provided by conversa-tions, experiences and encounter' (Greenfield, 2000: 63). In summary, then, talking with, talking to, and talking around babies matters enormously to their language and cognitive growth.

'How do permutations of a handful of different sounds . . . make it possible to enter into a relationship with the things and people around us, even perhaps to understand something about ourselves? How does language say what it says?' (Frayne, 2006: 273)

It is important to acknowledge the role of affect in thinking about how babies are introduced to, respond to, and create around them a world of talk. It has been suggested by research that just as babies are intrinsically motivated to learn, then so too are their mothers intrinsically motivated to impart knowl-edge – and this is biologically determined (Gopnik, 2009). Although perhaps this may, with notable exceptions, be a natural occurrence between parents and their babies, this same motivation may not always exist between caregivers in daycare settings outside the home and the babies in their care. Issues of attachment are discussed elsewhere in this book, but in the context of this chapter it may be important to consider further the idea of 'mutual attunement' between adults and babies and the need for babies to be recipients of 'consistent and close adult attention ... and playful communication' (Trevarthen et al., 2003: 40). In our Baby Room Project, we were concerned that the benefits of intimacy, of close interactions and the provision of opportunities for expression and conversation between adults and babies, were not always evident. Of course, it may be that when observed or filmed a natural shyness in enacting such roles took over. However, our evidence challenged a common assumption made that young, female practitioners will intuitively perform 'maternal-like' interactions with babies. We feel confident from our study that this simply cannot be assumed and needs to be addressed in training and continuing professional development opportunities. While we witnessed few intimate 'speech acts', there was an abundance of evidence that the practitioner participants in our study demonstrated, and indeed appeared to feel, affection towards the babies in their care. They talked about the importance of 'cuddling' babies and expressed concern in their professional development sessions with us that in one nursery the practitioners were not allowed to kiss the babies (for further discussions of this, see Powell and Goouch, 2012). Other research evidence points to the fact that 'affectionate touch occurs more frequently than smiling and affectionate words' (Dineen, 2009: 171). In the project, there seemed to be an anomaly – that is, we were working with lively, young women who conversed freely with us and with each other in the context of the project settings; however, in practice, this same liveliness was not always apparent. We began to understand that, even without our presence or the presence of a camera, they seemed to feel embarrassed or self-conscious about talking to a baby who could not 'talk', in the conventional sense, to them. We wondered also whether the practitioners had a model of this kind of talk practice with babies in their professional experience or in their own lives. It also appeared, as mentioned earlier from the project's evidence, that a rather rigid focus on routines and daily functional practices seemed to inhibit if not prohibit the need for close talk interactions and the development of opportunities for sustained speech acts. Although the project work prompted participants to consider talk to be rather more important than they had previously thought, for example:

> I now encourage my colleagues to provide time to talk to babies ... and listen.
> It's understanding how important talking to the babies is.

> (Final evaluations, December 2011)

there were examples in the project of participants who seemed naturally and without hesitation or inhibition to initiate and respond to babies. In this interview, which took place in her baby room, one participant both talked about and demonstrated her responses:

I try to get down to his level when I speak to him, yes physically on his level, either sitting or laying down on the floor with him. And with talking, if he is babbling, I still talk to him but sometimes adding the odd babble in, mimicking what he says . . . [using a] soft voice, playful voice or excited. When he is sad being reassuring to him, in your voice you can tell.

(Practitioner interview, October 2011)

These example were, however, quite rare. In her study of the ability of relationship training for caregivers to enhance young children's learning and language, Dineen (2009) found that 'the evidence is overwhelming: training for caregiving does matter' and her work demonstrated 'a direct correlation between relational pedagogy, sensitivity of carers and the developmental potential of young children' (p. 182).

To really focus on understanding the importance of talk practices in daycare settings, a reading of Bakhtin's assertions, alongside those of the neuroscientists cited earlier, is helpful:

The word in language is half someone else's. It becomes 'one's own' only when the speaker populates it with his own intention, his own accent, when he appropriates the word, adapting it to his own semantic and expressive intention. Prior to this moment of appropriation, the word does not exist in a neutral and impersonal language (it is not, after all, out of a dictionary that the speaker gets his words!) but rather it exists in other people's mouths, in other people's contexts, serving other people's intentions: it is from there that one must take the word, and make it one's own.

(Bakhtin, 1981: 294)

Ranging across multi-disciplinary theories, then, provides us with clues towards an appropriate pedagogy to support and enrich the language abilities and potential of babies and young children. The 'appropriation' of language, from other people's words and born out of other people's worlds, is the way in which babies find, store, and re-create language use.

The Baby Room Project, together with the range of research evidence offered above, seems to indicate that a number of conditions need to be present for baby room practice to meet the needs of curious, pattern-forming, prototype-storing, causal map-makers and, essentially, developing meaning-makers. These include:

- a non-parent adult with whom to bond;
- opportunities to scrutinize, learn about, and memorize her face and voice;

- time for that adult to pay close attention to that baby;
- time for that baby to pay close attention to that adult;
- a geographical space that allows for the scrutiny and attention to occur on roughly equal ground;
- endless opportunities to share conversations.

Furthermore, the kinds of encounters listed here need to occur consistently so that a close familiarity can be developed. This does not need to be at the exclusion of all other adults and babies, but will underpin other relationships. This form of attachment – and we know from the previous chapter that babies can form attachments to a range of people as well as their mothers – will facilitate opportunities to develop language knowledge and use. One of the constraints to creating such constructive relationships appears to be the limited time that may be allotted to it. As stated in previous chapters, baby room practitioners frequently feel their day to be overtaken by 'tasks', which, they believe, preclude them from engaging with babies in the ways they would ideally like. For example, in evaluation responses we heard participants say, when asked how the project had influenced their relationships with babies:

> I now sometimes question what I do and who it actually benefits.
> . . . more time me 'playing' with the babies and paperwork can wait!
> . . . talk – lots of talking and singing.
> . . . providing more time to spend one-to-one with the babies that have just started to settle them in and get to know them.
> I now spend longer time on the floor.
> (Practitioner evaluations, December 2011)

These kinds of responses imply that this approach to their work with babies had not previously been expected of them. In research that sought to explore the notion of 'relational pedagogy', Oates and Sanders investigated what they described as 'quality encounters' between adults and young learners. They worked with students to help them understand the 'little spaces', the 'in-between communication zone' in their attempts to enrich interactions towards the creation of quality encounters (Oates and Sanders, 2009: 187). The premise leading this project was that 'working in the little spaces with children can promote values of thoughtfulness and sensitivity' (p. 189). From the evidence in our study, we felt that the opportunities to capitalize on the 'little spaces' in routine and functional tasks were often missed. That is, practitioners' burden of a task-centred practice, on which their efficiency and effectiveness rested and was measured, overcame any desire they may have initially held to attend to relationships. This relational aspect of their pedagogy then fitted around, rather than being integral to, their tasks. Through this kind of project engagement, it is possible to help practitioners to redirect their gaze, without neglecting routine tasks of changing, feeding, and resting babies. However, there exists a clear need for initial training in this area of developing a reflective view of the relational aspect of baby room work (Dineen, 2009; Oates and Sanders, 2009) as well as appropriate continuing professional development for managers and owners of nurseries as well as those practising in baby rooms (see Nutbrown, 2012b). The support of babies to listen to, appropriate, and intentionally employ the words they encounter in their lived experiences in baby rooms seems to depend in large part on the knowledge and understanding of the practitioners (and their managers) of the need to develop rich, affective encounters with babies with whom they are familiar and who have developed a trusting relationship with these 'non-parent' adults. These encounters may be incidental to, or integral to, the tasks and operations of the day-to-day baby room experience.

How can we know the dancer from the dance? (W.B. Yeats, 1994)

Amidst a 'circulation of global governing discourses' (Bloch et al., 2003: 226) and in an age in which governments seem to be working towards the creation of single frameworks, a 'one-size-fits-all' approach to education and schooling, Alexander has argued for a 'dialogic curriculum' and the need for 'dialogue both about and in education; that is, both educational and pedagogic dialogue' (Alexander, 2008: 138). In the Baby Room Project, we argue for a third dialogic strand that incorporates opportunities for baby room practitioners to theorize their practice, to engage in reflective exchanges; one which facilitates the kinds of dialogic encounters that mirror the equality of engagement that is argued for all learners and teachers. While in some ways this argument is similar to that incorporating the pedagogic practices of Reggio Emilia, described as:

> a form of deconstructive pragmatism . . . a continuous struggle to problematise the inclusions and exclusions on which their own professional competence and authority is based in order to open up for new possibilities.
>
> (Dahlberg, 2003: 277)

in the project, the participants valued in particular the opportunities they were given to talk, to participate in professional gossip and to listen to, re-present and discuss ways of working. Discussion in relation to their own practice identity was frequent in these examples of 'deconstructive pragmatism', combined with a struggle as 'novice problematizers' to reflect on their

constructions of children, childhood and their notions of family. In the same way that we understand that extensive exposure to talk practices and language influences speech production in babies, so we began to understand that the ways in which we constructed discourse in relation to the worth of baby room practice, of the significance of being in a position to care for the most precious thing in a parent's life, began to have an impact on participants' own discursive levels. At the beginning of the project, the language used to describe their status included feeling 'the lowest of the low'; by the end of the project, the nature of their descriptive language relating to their role had changed somewhat:

> Makes you think how important our role is as prime carer when parents have left baby in our care.
> It has reinforced my belief that I play a very important role in the babies' education and care, and that this is acknowledged.
> Realization of the importance of your role, how much my input into a child's life can affect them.

(Final evaluation, 2012)

Smith's claims that the ability to think 'depends on the company we keep . . . on the way we perceive ourselves, which depends on the way other people treat us', and 'if you don't have a language you can't talk' (Smith, 1992: 125), are particularly relevant to our project but also to the more general field of nursery and baby room work. In the broad, widely accepted notion that work with babies and very young children requires little intellectual engagement and consists generally of only physically demanding and routine tasks, how practitioners are perceived and how they construct their own self-worth in relation to their practice seems of little consequence. The work is seen as being of low status and so those who carry out the work also have low status. This is reflected in the qualifications required of early childhood practitioners, which has been reported to the Nutbrown Review as less than that required to look after animals (Nutbrown, 2012b). Through the project work, participants were provided with the opportunity to draw on both the 'landscape of action' and the 'landscape of consciousness' (Bruner, 1986). It was through this 'duality of landscape' that they were able to reflect both on the pragmatics of their work with babies as well as their understandings of their work – their actions and their re-actions. Their initial feelings of voicelessness were transformed as they began to feel that their identities were not only shaped by their occupation but also that they had the ability to shape both their own understandings and their future practice. Rather than feeling themselves to be victims of policy, Ofsted, business practices, and others' ideologies, as a result of 'learning in companionship' (Whitehead, 2009) the participants in the project were helped to narrate their identities, their understandings, and their work with babies. Vygotsky describes this as the difference between 'signalling' functions and 'signifying' functions in his analysis of children's speech development and their search for words. It would appear that this 'signalling to signifying' development can equally be applied to adult learners as through the project community, a trusting group of participants, they struggled together to find words to both describe and to explain their actions and responses in the stories of their practice. The project did not seek to define practice or to construct a 'governing discourse' of any kind but instead to create a dialogic opportunity to enable participants to separate out who they were in their care of babies, what they thought they were doing with babies from their perceptions of the prescriptions for practice that surrounded them. In this way, the tunes to which they 'danced' became familiar tunes that they understood through shared analysis and to which they contributed through the stories they told which helped to shape their future actions. The power of dialogue – 'a radical dialogue that does not resolve into a monologue' (Dahlberg, 2003: 281) or a scripted pedagogy instead provides opportunities for practitioners to learn to 'stutter', and to develop 'a constant critique and reflective attitude' (Dahlberg, 2003: 284).

6   Environments
Places and spaces for babies

Exploring environments provides another opportunity to examine notions of quality and the measures used to determine quality provision for babies in daycare, not just in the UK but also in other geographical and other cultural contexts. Alongside 'quality' the idea of 'a rich environment' needs to be interrogated, with work from neuroscience as well as other developmental, educational, and socio-cultural perspectives employed to develop deeper understanding of the key issues. In this chapter, we present research to explore the idea of baby rooms, the environmental factors that exist in daycare settings, and issues that limit or constrain the development of baby room environments. We also critically explore key influences on daycare environments, the impact of environments on babies, and babies' impact on their environments.

Understanding environments as crucial influences on development and learning has been an aspect of increasing professional interest in the Baby Room Project. The 'environment' is a wide-ranging term and incorporates issues of physical space, material resources, people and interactions, as well as consideration of social and emotional factors. The provision of spaces and places in which babies live and grow makes a difference to the ways in which they develop and the potential impact of affective partners in their growth and development. In experiments with rats, neuroscience research shows us that even adult rats when placed in an enriched environment are found to have more 'branching of the brain cells' than those in control groups:

> That's because even in adults, the more you stimulate the brain, the more it develops the potential for making connections . . . Its worth pointing out that an under-stimulating environment for children, given what we know about the human brain, would be ethically questionable.
>
> (Greenfield, 2000: 21)

This argument is often challenged by those observing attempts to enhance brain functioning in very young infants, particularly in the USA, through programmes designed to stimulate them in particular ways (for example, Baby Einstein, Baby Mozart). The argument, however, is clear. There is a difference between a bare, uneventful, silent environment with few, if any interactions and the kinds of environments proposed by Greenfield that awaken a baby's brain to possibilities. The research undertaken by neuroscientists indicates that 'there is a threshold of environmental richness below which a deprived environment could harm a baby's brain' (Blakemore and Frith, 2005: 33).

A room of their own

In 2008/9, when the idea of the Baby Room Project first emerged, interested colleagues expressed surprise that 'rooms for babies' existed at all. They frequently employed metaphors and talked about baby rooms as 'waiting rooms' or 'luggage racks' and some used the term now often employed by those discussing care for the elderly – 'warehouses' for babies while parents worked. Whereas for some in society the notion of babies under 12 months being in any kind of daycare is an anathema, for others it simply means that babies are mostly separated from older children under 3 years into a room of their own. The reality is that, mostly although not exclusively for financial reasons, there are babies from as young as 6 weeks of age who are in formal, full-time daycare for up to 45 hours each week. The requirements for babies in daycare, however, are rarely publicly discussed. Even in the recently revised *Early Years Foundation Stage* (EYFS) published by the UK's Department for Education, 'babies' are hardly mentioned, although a require-ment is made that there should be a separate baby room for children under 2 years (DfE, 2012). Whether or not babies are cared for in out-of-home contexts depends to a large extent on parental leave policies (OECD, 2006). Although the experiences of babies in daycare have not been well researched (see David et al., 2003), the wide-ranging review of research undertaken in Scotland delivers some clear messages in relation to the care of babies under 12 months:

> The large body of research on the socio-emotional development of infants gives clear support to common wisdom. No infant under 6 months can gain confidence and understanding in a large group of infants with a small proportion of caregivers. Infants require consistent and close adult attention, for rest, protection and nurtur-ance and to benefit from playful communication . . . Moreover, even infants under 6 months are affected by the familiarity and consist-ency of the environment. Beyond six months, the identity and

interest of the partner becomes even more critical as the infant tries to grasp sharing of rituals and imitates expressive actions.

(Trevarthen et al., 2003: 41–2)

What are we to learn from these kinds of messages from research findings? The picture becomes slightly less than straightforward in the UK, but also in other Western European countries and in the USA, New Zealand, and Australia, when contemporary policies demand parents' employment, impose welfare cuts, and plan limits to state support for parents who stay at home to care for their children. Parents are often in a position where 'a combination of the wish to be available to children when they are small, to share their lives and experiences, and a dissatisfaction with either the levels of the quality of care provision, and anxiety about the way they themselves are perceived . . . makes the struggle unattractive' (David, 1999: 147). However, in spite of the difficulties, the frustrations, and the emotional struggle, the economic reality of the twenty-first century means that more than 40 per cent of babies and children under the age of 2 years are being cared for by people who are not their parents. Given this situation, what does constitute 'quality' or 'richness' in relation to the environments in which babies will spend large parts of their lives? Is there a universally recognized 'high-quality' environment that has been acknowledged to benefit babies and provide 'protection and nurturance'?

Perspectives on quality in environments for babies

In the UK, the regulatory body Ofsted claims that their overarching aim during their inspection visits is to ask: 'what is it like for a child here?' They include in their requirements 'a highly stimulating and welcoming environment', high-quality resources, and 'accommodation well suited to its purpose' as indicators of outstanding quality of provision. Additionally, most guides to quality, including that of Ofsted, focus explicitly on 'what' happens in nurseries, with an emphasis on routines or other structural issues, such as ratios, staff qualities, health and safety, as well as the adequate provision of space. This kind of focus has drawn some harsh criticism of the nature of some of the research influencing practice decisions, which has focused attention on 'quantitative methodologies' within 'a positivist research paradigm' (Fenech, 2011).

> 'Quality' is presented in the research as an objective construct that can be known via quantitative measures and statistical analyses. What contributes to 'quality ECEC' are those aspects that can be observed and standardised; operationalised using (generally) global, structural and/or process indicators; and measured quantitatively.
>
> (Fenech, 2011: 109)

The implication is that only those aspects of care that can be simply described and are easily measurable are useful indicators of quality in ECEC.

Within such systems it is invariably difficult to capture complex, subtle or 'more nuanced' (Fenech, 2011) aspects of care and provision. In the UK, many local authorities who are responsible for guiding provision appear to have adopted the ratings guides 'ECERS/ECERS-R' (Early Childhood Environment Rating Scale/ Revised) and 'ITERS/ITERS-R' (Infant and Toddler Environment Rating Scale/Revised), which originated in the USA, and have introduced these to settings as a definitive guide to establishing quality in provision. A high profile has been afforded to these scales, as ECERS and ECERS-E (Extension) were employed by the Effective Pre-school and Primary Education (EPPE) Project to demonstrate quality (Sylva and Roberts, 2010). However, in the EPPE Project, the measures were used to demonstrate that 'effective' pre-school attendance could be linked to outcomes, particularly academic attainment, again measured in a particularly contested way, that is through National Assessment Tests. Fenech argues that while these kinds of measurement tools may illuminate some elements of quality, others may be hidden in 'blind spots' as a result and makes reference, for example, to the scant attention given to children's gross motor development and the lack of attention to spiritual, moral, and ethical development. As a result, the British government's focus on English and maths receives close attention in relation to the effectiveness of the environment provided to promote these 'subjects' and a top-down impact of this can be felt in the ways in which the environments in nurseries and daycare settings are measured. Furthermore and as a result of this emphasis, reference to provision for babies is frequently missing from these judgements (Fenech, 2011; Mathers et al., 2012). A further difficulty with reliance on external quality measures that employ rating scales is in their reliability and trustworthiness. In a study by Mathers, Singler and Karemaker, which offered a comparison of outcomes from the use of ECERS and ITERS and grades from the regulatory body Ofsted, they found that 'there was little obvious association between the grades awarded by Ofsted for the whole setting and quality for children under 30 months, as assessed by the ITERS-R. For example, settings graded as outstanding by Ofsted often achieved the lowest scores on the ITERS-R' (Mathers et al., 2012: 73)

As the opposite was also found to be true, that those achieving high scores on the ITERS-R scales were frequently observed to be unsatisfactory by Ofsted, some providers would be forgiven for being confused by these somewhat conflicting results. While lists of characteristics of an appropriate environment for babies and very young children may be useful as guidance in setting up and maintaining provision, on their own these can only offer a baseline from which those practising in baby rooms and nurseries can develop their environments in accordance with their understanding of the needs of the children, their families, and the communities in which they work. In the above study, it was suggested that a broad basket of tools should be employed to create an audit of quality. This, of course, demands a level of knowledge and commitment from practitioners and their managers in relation to child development as well as the social circumstances of the setting. It also requires commitment to the 'here and now' for babies, that is, consideration needs to be given to what the babies' physical, social, emotional, and cognitive needs are frequently and of the moment, and how these can best be met. These kinds of considerations will better overcome the problem of 'blind spots' that so-called objective measures often produce and which are frequently informed or led by national policies rather than informed by local, community or individual contexts.

Parents are frequently quoted as saying that the physical environment is less important than the qualities of the people caring for their child, although warmth, cleanliness, and safety are terms often used to describe quality, when first making a choice of childcare provision, with 'warmth' referring to interactions and relationships. Local authority workers, though, expressed concern that resources and a high-quality environment did not always lead to high-quality care – 'there is no point in having all the gear and no idea' (Mathers et al., 2012: 41) – and that some articulate managers and owners were able to 'talk the talk' and tick boxes effectively, that is, they learned to play the game of accounting for their environments. The real difficulty, for parents and other visitors to settings, is that they are able only to capture a snapshot in time and more frequent visits and observations would perhaps allow for a better informed and fully formed picture of provision. Combined with this problem is the difficulty of really understanding what it is that parents require from daycare. In the Baby Room Project, interviews with parents initially produced rather nebulous responses, 'I just want her to be safe', 'I want to go to work knowing I can trust them to look after her', but after prompting included safe places, routines, people, and the meeting of basic needs. One parent talked of the importance of their baby being 'well looked after in physical terms' and others talked of the benefits of being in the company of other babies, the social aspect of care as paramount.

In the first phase of the Baby Room Project, the managers/owners were asked at an initial interview what they considered to be 'the perfect baby room'. There were some common features to the responses, including 'safety' and ease of access to an outside area, preferably a garden, dedicated to the babies. Others mentioned the importance of care for parents and families and talked of ease of parking and access for parents, a 'parent-friendly' access, a drop-off room, a lobby, a space for parents to sit while they drop off their baby. Some provided their own 'wish list', including a dedicated laundry room, a milk kitchen, a bigger space altogether or a purpose-built space. Areas for sleeping and changing were topical, with different opinions expressed about the need for open or closed changing areas in relation to safeguarding issues, and the arguments for and against dedicated sleep rooms rather than sleep spaces not closed from the rest of the environment. Light, low-level windows, sensory areas, safe crawling/exploring spaces, and a range of surfaces were also features of this group's ideal baby room environment. Some participants' visions included access to older children, rather than babies being completely removed from sight or sound of siblings or older children, including some they might know from their community.

In early discussions with practitioners who participated in the project, many were at first rather overwhelmed by the opportunity to create an ideal baby room or to consider which resources they would happily lose or which they would guard and keep. This may have been because their experience is not that of power or responsibility or choice in their working lives in nurseries and therefore they were not ready or equipped to respond to the independence that this activity offered. Another reason for their reticence may be a lack of knowledge in relation to the range of needs of babies. Also at this stage in the project, the participants were very much focused on themselves as a prime resource for babies and were finding difficulty in projecting themselves into the category of 'environment'. Further prompting provoked discussions in relation to toys, storage, change and sleep spaces, cots and nests. Outside the intimacy of the project sessions, later interviews with managers revealed that some practitioners had returned from development sessions to review and evaluate their rooms, that they had come back to 're-look' at the baby room environment in which they worked; they had begun to 'reflect on what's important', to look at how it could be developed. In one notable example of a large room that was subdivided by a low partition to separate babies and children of different ages, the practitioner had noticed that the partition had been chewed where toddling infants had hoisted themselves up on to it so that they could watch the older children. This had not been previously noted and now her suggestion of glass bricks to form the division has become part of the new development plan for the room. Some of the participant practitioners were surprised by and interested in the fact that the physical environment could have an impact on the babies in their care.

Research also seemed to have 'a voice' in determining the environments for babies in daycare. Some members of the practitioner group, as well as managers, had 'absorbed' notions or aspects of research from what was going on around them, the media or other rarely provided professional development opportunities. One example of this is the idea of black and white backgrounds, toys and resources for babies. The rationale for this is that babies apparently have blurred vision and can distinguish sharp contrasts more easily. Although the research surrounding this element of growth and development of sight is focused on babies in the first days and weeks of their life when they are not in daycare, the result has been that many nurseries and particularly baby rooms have areas swathed in black and white fabric with toys to match. Another example is from training to support 'heuristic play', following which only natural materials are included in some settings, with all plastic and man-made toys and resources taken away, resulting in a sometimes colourless environment. In both examples, the origins of the information can be traced to valid sources. However, in translation and with the best of intentions, a literal interpretation has frequently resulted that creates environments devoid of colour, variety, and choice. In both examples, commercial companies have been swift to capitalize on the goodwill of those working with babies, and catalogues and marketing materials frequently begin with phrases such as 'it is widely acknowledged that . . .', 'research has shown that . . .', 'use of these materials will pave the way to brain cell connections . . .', making it difficult for those without access to primary sources of research or affirming/challenging support for practice to withstand strong market forces. However, there is no doubt that significantly more attention needs to be given to baby rooms:

> banks, shops and restaurants pay huge sums to interior designers to create a visual environment which is attractive to customers during their brief visits. Yet we are often content for children to spend their most formative years surrounded by ugliness and clutter.
>
> (Goldschmied and Jackson, 2004: 21)

The low status of nursery care, the low levels of investment over time in the built and resource environment, often results in the nursery and the baby room in particular 'making do' with low-cost or shabby environments. In our project, there was a stark contrast between some settings in community or church halls, nissen huts or dis-used classrooms, and those in purpose-built settings with glass walls, underfloor heating, and extensive resources. Goldschmied and Jackson claim that in other countries, particularly Italy, more emphasis is given to the visual nature of the environment in which babies and young children grow and learn.

'An amiable environment'

In the Reggio Emilia tradition, in Northern Italy, there is an attempt to create 'an amiable environment, where children, families and teachers feel at ease' (Edwards et al., 1998: 63). There, the claim is that the physical characteristics of a setting reveal how children are valued and that the environments in Reggio Emilia are 'noteworthy . . . not only because they are aesthetically and intellectually stimulating, but because they convey a respect for the interests, rights, needs and capacities of those who use that space' (p. 266). This level of respect is a timely reminder that not only are babies spending large amounts of time in baby rooms, but so too are their carers and the wellbeing of the caring adults is of utmost importance to the wellbeing of those being cared for.

Equally, the focus on interests as well as capacities indicates the importance of scaffolding or supporting the possibilities of encounter between a child and an environment or material resource.

The 'space' or environment is considered in Reggio Emilia to be an additional educator; that is, that children learn from their surroundings from the earliest age:

> We value space because of its power to organise, promote pleasant relationships among people of different ages, create a handsome environment, provide changes, promote choices and activity, and its potential for sparking all kinds of social, affective and cognitive learning. All of this contributes to a sense of well-being and security in children. We also think that the space has to be a sort of aquarium that mirrors the ideas, values, attitudes and cultures of the people who live within it.
>
> (Malaguzzi, 1998: 177)

The potential for meeting and creating relationships with children of different ages is given prominence in Reggio Emilia settings and the rather distinctive 'piazzas' or meeting places are evident in purpose-built infant/toddler settings there. These areas are often surrounded by smaller hubs or areas that are specifically resourced for different aged babies and young children but they are not containers or sealed environments. Another feature of some of the preschools is the different textured and sloping surfaces on which babies can crawl and explore. While Goldschmied and Jackson talk of carpeted surfaces as being 'essential' for children who have started to stand and step, on a visit to a New Zealand setting, a conversation with a nursery teacher revealed interesting observations of a very young, just standing child, as she stepped barefooted from a carpeted surface to a hard surface, treading on the shiny edging material as she did so. The teacher remarked that the child was 'experiencing the world through her senses, through her body, reading her world through her feet' (personal conversation with teacher) and had noted that she stepped repeatedly across the same section, looking down as she went, illustrating well Malaguzzi's idea of the educational potential of the environment.

Very young babies' requirements for their physical environment are rather different and must service the need for 'closeness and nurturing exchanges' (Edwards et al., 1998: 174). Indeed, it is claimed that 'beneficial care for infants in the first year will require an environment that resembles a home with affectionate and reliable company and periods of quiet, free of conflict' (Trevarthen et al., 2003: 42). Pillows, soft nests, snuggling spaces, small mattresses, and curling up spaces have been identified by the project participants as significant features of ideal practice and some versions of these are often found in baby rooms across the world. The project participants, as well as the researchers cited here, frequently talked of attempts to create an environment that demonstrated 'homeliness', 'a homely atmosphere' or 'a home-like space'. Although in practice this is sometimes reduced to curtains at a window, an armchair or settee and cushions, it raises the question of whose home it is intended to represent. However, the intention perhaps could be interpreted as the creation of a non-institutional atmosphere, labelled for convenience as 'more homely'. From their observations, Singer and de Haan (2007) claim that very young babies in childcare centres use other babies in the room – for imitation, eye contact, and communication purposes. Indeed, just as Newson and Newson (1979) talked of mothers becoming a baby's first plaything and their first 'play-mate', so in daycare contexts other babies form a human resource, particularly from the age of 6 months when their body movements have developed a new vigour and variety and as they develop more control (Trevarthen, 1998).

Adult purposes, adult spaces

While in theory it is relatively easy to conjure up an image of a soft, cosy, interactive, sometimes quiet, ideal baby room, it is often the case that such spaces do not exist in practice and the rhetoric remains just that. The dominance of routines and structures, created perhaps for either commercial, safeguarding or management reasons, may overcome the needs of very young babies and children, or may create conflict in the minds of those practising. For example, our project participants were concerned about a high-profile media report of a nursery worker abusing children in her care in closed room spaces away from public gaze. This case resulted in many practitioners preferring to change babies in full sight of colleagues, in open spaces. Unfortunately, this created a conflict as respect for the child's privacy became secondary and adults' needs prevailed:

> This thing about CRB checks and the CCTV cameras. I trust the staff who work here. Why should we need to prop a door open when we change a baby's nappy? Somebody, perhaps a visitor or parent, might walk past and see and then there's no dignity or privacy for the baby.
> (Participant interview, May 2010)

Two other aspects of the routine lives of babies and their carers created potential tensions – sleep and mealtimes – and these will be considered separately.

Sleep

There are a number of elements that contribute to the health and wellbeing of babies and infants. Sleep is important as it 'influences the manner in which we acquire and maintain new skills, how we remember information and our ability to think creatively' (Blakemore and Frith, 2005). Incredibly, neuroscientists, brain researchers, and sleep scientists have been able to discover some of the important ways in which the brain and body operate during sleep periods. Researchers claim that brain and body cells become detoxified during sleep, body tissues and cells can be restored and, as the brain is still active during sleep, 'memories can be laid down about experiences and information encountered during the day' (Blakemore and Frith, 2005: 173). Babies sleep for approximately 15 hours a day. However, the sleep/wake patterns vary and these variations are most acute across different cultural communities. For example, in the UK, the USA, and other western cultures, it is often for reasons of convenience and for 'a chance to disengage from continuous care' (Super and Harkness, 1998: 41) that babies are regulated to sleep at particular times. Super and Harkness compared these patterns of behaviour with those of families in western Kenya, where a baby's wakefulness did not disrupt the everyday activities in which mothers were involved or 'a sibling caretaker, a co-wife or another relative' was available to provide support in the care of a child. In the Baby Room Project, sleep patterns and the regulation of sleep, as well as sleep arrangements and resources were high-profile concerns and frequently referred to by the participants. One particular area of tension seemed to be that parents and family members often instructed practitioners to keep babies awake during the day to ensure sleepiness at night. Others insisted their babies were put in a cot to sleep. The contexts of influences on daycare practices are developed more fully in Chapter 8. Although reported some years ago, Goldschmied and Jackson's (1994) claim that they saw baby rooms almost entirely taken up with cots, while not common, may still be the case in some areas, with somewhat rigid routines of 'putting' babies to sleep, particularly after lunch, commonplace. Some of the daycare settings in the project had separate sleep rooms, while others had a few cots and many more nests or baskets that were distributed around the room either at distinct 'sleep times' or when a baby or babies appeared to need them. The development of these kinds of resources have been helpful in enabling more flexible practices, although in one example from the project, the effect of underfloor heating on babies sleeping in these informal nests was occasionally seen to be harmful.

Mealtimes

Whether the baby room contained three babies or many more, the routinization of mealtimes invariably took place and lunch, which seemed to arrive usually in baby rooms at 11.30 am, was often observed to be a most stressful occasion. In some very large and busy baby rooms, the babies were divided between those who were able to sit upright at a very low table, those who sat in high chairs, and those who were bottle-fed. The timing of meal events was sometimes also problematic as it took a considerable amount of time to ensure that each child was safely in their place, which often resulted in the first few children being seated for a long time before any food appeared. In such rooms, the proceedings became almost 'a conveyor belt' system, with few, if any, opportunities for sociable chatter, reassurance or kindness, although where key person systems operate this can be slightly ameliorated. It is easy to appreciate how mealtimes become a routine to be completed as quickly and as easily as possible and a sense of 'institutional rush' (Goldschmied and Jackson, 1994: 170) created around babies and young children who are just beginning to learn the importance of food and the management of their senses as well as develop their fine motor skills. However, in the same way that the challenge of changing many babies' nappies during the course of each day cannot be under-estimated, nor can the challenge of waiting and watching and supporting babies as they slowly wade through their meals, in the knowledge that the routines continue and clearing away, cleaning and then resting children needs to be achieved. The possible outcome is that babies are recipients of speedy actions, taken for expedience rather than care as in the following salutary example:

> Peter, a child who was partly feeding himself with his fingers and partly being fed, had food around his mouth; the adult scraped it off with the spoon. This was repeated many times, and the observer noted that each time the child winced slightly. In the group room meeting staff tried doing it to each other to see how it felt. As a result they vowed never to do it to a child again.
>
> (Goldschmied and Jackson, 1994: 171)

Through the eyes of the child . . .

As babies and young children begin relating to both people and to things (Hobson, 2002), the environments created need to reflect their readiness to explore the places, people, and materials surrounding them. Babies appear 'to be tuned to learn from, with and about first the people and the cultural environment around them, followed by the material environment – they come into the world primed to be curious, competent learners' (David, 2005: 34). By the time babies are 3–4 months old, their brains have developed sufficiently to allow them to have a level of control and to commit voluntary acts, moving their head and their gaze to follow movement. Their own rolling movements, then crawling and then standing positions allow them to see the world from different perspectives, which in turn supports other aspects of babies' development (David et al., 2003; Karmiloff-Smith, 1994). In the project, to support their understanding of the perspective of the world babies tended to have from their position on the floor, participants were asked to lay down on the baby room floor themselves, to view the world from a baby's perspective. One participant stated the following:

> I was interested in what Kathy had said about getting a child's eye view. So the other day I had little Emily laying on a mat because she's tiny and I laid down next to her. I remember [manager] coming in and saying, 'are you comfortable down there?' and I said, 'well I'm at her level' [laughing] . . . it probably did look like I wasn't doing anything. I lay there talking to her laying down instead of me sitting up over her . . . as soon as I lay down beside her her head turned, we were sort of practically nose to nose and her hand was coming out and touching my nose and poking my eyes whereas before I suppose she couldn't reach me from down there 'cos I was just over her but being there really contacting her was quite nice. It just makes you think of those little things just a bit more.
>
> (Practitioner interview, May 2010)

This kind of exploratory play, with the opportunity to develop reciprocity, seems to be essential for babies to define the familiar, to interrogate the less familiar, to develop new knowledge, and to establish a close understanding of the important adults in their lives. Exploring people, and things, enables babies to 'map their spatial world' (David et al., 2003: 125), their place within it, but also, through early experiences and encounters as children's brains create causal theories of the world, maps of how the world works. And these theories allow children to envisage new possibilities, and to imagine and pretend that the world is different (Gopnik, 2009: 21).

The process of 'mapping' the world requires 'guided participation' (Rogoff, 1990) by knowledgeable adults who are able to present and re-present aspects of that world to the babies in their care, demonstrate possibilities, and to sensitively scaffold babies' explorations and attempts at independence. A closeness, a 'benevolence' (Rogoff, 1990) in approach is required of adults as babies navigate their way towards intentionality and self-sufficiency. Understanding the nature of this complex, tentative, and often layered support requires a deep level of knowledge of how babies develop and learn, as well as experience gained through close observation.

> I suppose before I probably thought the babies don't need as much 1 to 1 as an older one; and it's like somebody was saying last week [at PD session], a child that's louder gets the attention, but a baby laying

there still under a mobile, they do still need that interaction with you as much as the other louder ones and as much as a 15- or 18-month old child.

(Practitioner interview, May 2010)

While project participants spoke of how they were often viewed as 'glorified babysitters', Trevarthen talks of the needs of babies to be supported by 'sensitive care in stable and peaceful relationships with a few adults . . . in responsive companionship' (Trevarthen et al., 2003: 31). Perhaps people do matter rather more than places in babies' lives. However, as babies construct their world maps, people need to be responsive partners in their journeys through the places and spaces they encounter on their route.

7 A few out-of-home truths
Paradigms and perspectives

In this chapter, we briefly summarize how people have theorized the child and the provision and practice we call ECEC, according to their different perspectives – or paradigms – both traditionally and as direct challenges to prevailing ideas. We will then explore where ideas – or constructs – about babies and/or baby rooms (daycare for babies) seem most closely aligned with one or more of these paradigms.

Taking a philosophical approach, we will try to unravel some of the complexities that stem from differing perspectives. Studies of society and social phenomena are shaped by people's beliefs about who we are and about the nature of 'being' (ontology) as well as about what knowledge is and where it comes from (epistemology). These ideas affect how people think about (the earliest part of) human life and the 'babies' we refer to in this book. We will explore how these perspectives continue to influence ideas about what a baby is, what he or she can or should do, and how research, policy, and practice evolves from or conforms to these theoretical positions, sometimes overtly supporting one perspective, at other times traversing or fusing together, intentionally or unconsciously, aspects of multiple paradigms.

It is common to encounter claims of (or for) a 'paradigm shift' in the thinking that informs ECEC. This refers to a now substantial body of work that challenges taken-for-granted ideas and affiliated social actions or practices as well as the ways these are re-presented (in words, images, and other symbolic forms). The word paradigm comes from the Latin and Greek words that mean 'pattern' and its use in relation to research and scholarship is attributed to the philosopher of science, Thomas Kuhn (Kuhn, 1996). Capra (1996: 6) describes a paradigm as,

> a constellation of concepts, values, perceptions and practices shared by a community which forms a particular vision of reality that is the basis of the way a community organizes itself.
>
> (cited in Huitt, 2011: 6)

Although there have been many different definitions of paradigm (see Mukherji and Albon, 2010: 10–11), the term continues to be used broadly to designate ontological and methodological orientations when used in social research. But as research within (and across) disciplines has evolved to represent a multitude of beliefs and practices, there is no single paradigm for all research. Consequently, it is possible for many paradigms to exist simultaneously, to conflict and compete with one another or to have quite different aims. Some researchers' ideas will claim or be used to reinforce particular views about knowledge and reality and may be 'mainstream' or marginal. Robinson and Jones Díaz have argued about paradigms, that

> The international field of early childhood education is currently experiencing a major challenge to the authority of many of the long-standing traditional theories and practices that have been utlilized in approaches to children and children's learning.
>
> (Robinson and Jones Díaz, 2006: 1).

Our own view is based on an assumption that there is an axiomatic relationship between what and how people think and what they do (and why); and that 'truths' about social institutions or structures, for example, 'the baby room' or 'ECEC', can come about through open and mutually respectful dialogic encounters. But we have a simultaneous concern that many of these social structures may continue to be 'reproduced' (Giddens, 1984) through collective actions or agency that are mediated by differing degrees of power. Consequently, this social reproduction becomes, '[t]he process through which the social order and hierarchies of power are perpetuated through institutions such as the family, schools and the military' (Robinson and Jones Díaz, 2006: 184) as well as the media. Although these structures may be socially constructed – a product of people's shared beliefs – they can seem to take on an 'objective' reality, to have a life of their own beyond the intersubjective imagination. Inglis and Thorpe (2012: 21) use the analogy of Dr. Frankenstein's monstrous creation to help explain this. They may then be seen to be a means of social control and domination by those perceived to have greater power. Some feminist writers have tried to expose the ways that particular 'discourses' help to strengthen the position of some people and weaken that of others in the early childhood field and their work falls under a critical, post-structural paradigm (see, for example, Canella, 1997; Farquhar and Fitzsimons, 2008; Osgood, 2012; Soto, 2000; Yelland, 2005). They try to show how the collective beliefs and actions of dominant groups are either accepted or rejected by people who are made less powerful and this can include women, childcare workers, people from 'working-class' or 'ethnic minority' groups, and babies and young children. How a society thinks about babies, children and infants, childhood and the relationships of these constructs to adults and adulthood are the 'constellations of concepts, values, perceptions and practices' that we will consider in the next section.

Ways of seeing 'the child'

> The young child goes through a . . . process as a 'candidate' member of the culture – and cultures vary in how they delineate that candidacy. If it is Original Sin that he carried into the world with him, then he is to be coerced from his stricken state. If he is of the Song of Innocence, another rule awaits. If he is a candidate for the organizational life, then perhaps Little League is the right acculturation instrument. No child is ever a tabula rasa in the eyes of the culture.
>
> (Bruner, 2000: x)

Bruner's idea that every baby's arrival in the world is met with culturally specific responses reflects the paradigm within which he works: socio-cultural constructivism. This is just one of several paradigms that orientate the ways that babies and children are viewed and treated – or theoretical positions from which these emerge – and indeed whether any distinction is made between different periods of human existence that give rise to terms such as 'infant', 'toddler', and 'baby'.

What is childhood?

Kehily (2008: 1) observed that,

> Different disciplines have developed different ways of approaching the study of children, using different research methods driven by a far from coherent set of research questions. For some disciplines (such as sociology and cultural studies) childhood as a concept is specifically addressed, while for other disciplines (such as psychology and education) the focus has been upon the child or children.

This idea extends beyond the research domains and into the public sphere and professional practice. Lowe (2009) suggested that contemporary ideas about the child and studies of children and childhood have been influenced by four major debates.

First, he identifies a dichotomy in fundamental views about the (moral) nature of children: being innately evil and in need of redemption (by adults) so they may grow into effective adults on the one hand; or being innately innocent and in need of protection from the world's corrupting influences on the other hand. The former was heavily influenced by Christianity in Europe and the latter by the Romantics of the eighteenth and nineteenth centuries, such as Jean-Jacques Rousseau and William Wordsworth.

> If a baby is a manifestation of Original Sin, then how do we behave towards him and what is our goal?

Second, he notes that differences of opinion were rooted in beliefs that childhood might be a social construction or a biological stage in the development of all human beings.

> If 'childhood' is simply a feature and function of our human biology, then it follows that children's development will follow identical patterns at any time and place anywhere in the world, be that in Edinburgh, Bogotá or Kuala Lumpur.

Third, he suggests the role that nature–nurture arguments have had in shaping ideas about children and childhood, asking for example, 'Are the differences and distinctions in male and female adult behaviour and the differing roles ascribed to them within society the result of differing hormones and a differing genetic endowment or are they the result of the social conditioning which takes place during the early years?' (Lowe, 2009: 25)

> Are girls innately better at caring than boys?

Fourth, he considers the interconnected roles of time and place in how childhood has been viewed throughout history in different contexts.

> We might recall the analyses made by Hoyles (1989), Hendrick (1990) and others of how 'the child' of developmental psychology and educational practices emerged at a political moment within industrialising societies when children and young people were becoming economically active, increasingly organised and therefore challenging – as are working children across the world today (Burman 2001: 11).

What is common to elements of each of these debates is the idea of universality or a common developmental trajectory as well as arguments against this perspective. In addition, there is the hint of correlation and causality between early experience and later outcomes. Lowe also acknowledges the significant contributions that social historians Philippe Ariès and Lloyd DeMause have made to considerations of childhood throughout (western) history. Ariès for suggesting that the concept of childhood was 'discovered' as a result of growing affluence that led to the possibility for a person's experiences (their treatment by others) during the first years of life to be qualitatively different from later years (Ariès, 1962). It should be noted that Ariès's work has been the subject of significant criticism from historians, as has the claim of some social scientists, partly using Ariès's ideas, that a 'new paradigm' of the sociology of childhood was created (Heywood, 2010). DeMause was hailed for the 'psychologizing' of childhood (Lowe, 2009: 24) and for suggesting that people's behaviour as adults can be explained by how they experienced childhood (DeMause, 1974). MacNaughton (2003) has similarly attributed many of the ideas that underpin attitudes to early childhood and provision for young children to major philosophical or scientific movements, which she groups as:

1) ideas about the child conforming to nature or culture (including maturation, behaviourist, and social learning theories);
2) ideas about the interaction between the child's nature and culture (including constructivist, psychodynamic, and neuroscientific theories); and
3) ideas about the child transforming and being transformed by culture and nature (which includes post-structuralists, critical race theorists and post-colonialists, as well as the social constructionists and postmodernists for whom knowledge is, 'non-universal, complex, contradictory and changing' and 'means giving up views of the child that may work against the values of those cultures that have been silenced through traditional Western developmental views of the child' (MacNaughton, 2003: 76–7).

MacNaughton then suggests that there are commonly held beliefs between proponents of the theories in the first two groups, which differ dramatically from the third. Blenkin and Kelly (2000) have criticized attempts to eradicate predominantly psychological concepts of the child – traditionally adopted by many educationalists – in favour of postmodern, sociology-derived constructs of an agentic child. In their view, the loss of the broad concept of infancy as a time of dependency and vulnerability has devalued and diminished educational aspects of provision for babies; and the deconstruction of idealized versions of childhood, naively conceived by those unsettling this discourse, has left what they believe to be a dangerous conceptual void where infants are concerned.

Paradigmatic bridges

Burman has criticized hegemonic and normalizing tendencies of developmental psychology. But she also laments the creation of dualisms such as constructivism-versus-postmodernism, which she sees as unhelpful for all

(Burman, 2001). She argues for a move away from the dominant, central positioning of developmental (or modernist) arguments and their construction as diametrically opposed to or deconstructed by other positions. The latter, she suggests, situate themselves more peripherally and with less agency to influence policy, for example, which leads to positioning the child in much the same way. The implication for us has been to consider a wide range of theoretical perspectives and to attempt to recognize how these may limit our understandings and by extension may also limit babies' experiences.

In another account that moves away from dualistic comparisons of the/a child, Judith Duncan noted that images of the child in the literature span:

1   The empty vessel
2   Labour market supply
3   Consumer
4   Lost and in need of protection
5   Becoming/being
6   Constructed according to the economic or social discourses of the time
7   Individuals with rights
8   Active co-constructors of knowledge, identity and culture
9   Capable and competent
10 Reflective of discourses, for example inherently evil or majority-world needy
11 National treasures (or not)

(Duncan, 2010: 102–4)

She is at pains to remind us that there exists a 'range of competing and conflicting images of children that any society can hold at any time, across time, and at particular given historical moments . . . [which] offer contested positions both for children's lives and for the adults who live and/or work with children' (ibid., p. 101).

It is possible for these conflicting perspectives to exist simultaneously and side-by-side within texts or discourses that at first glance may appear uniform, such as the EYFS. This can happen when a range of perspectives is drawn upon to create what becomes a patchwork document, when there is inattention to the underlying epistemological and ontological ideas and their implications (Powell, 2010), or when post-dualistic attempts are made to reconcile difference. We have attempted such a reconciliation in our discussion of babies' contexts of influence (Chapter 8), which adopts a critical lens to reflect on helpful features of Bronfenbrenner's bioecological model. Carmen Dalli (2010) has called for a 'critical ecology' of the early childhood education profession, which we have interpreted in our own way in the explorations of baby rooms shared in this book and through our efforts to raise the profile and status of the work in other ways.

Since the UK ratified the UN Convention on the Rights of the Child (UNCRC United Nations, 1989) in 1990, there has been a growing discourse of children's rights in childhood studies, policies, and provision for children. But this 'new paradigm' for childhood is not without contention. First, the measures put in place to support the implementation of Articles of the UNCRC (such as the right to education, to have their views heard, to leisure time) are based on a legal discourse that promotes a perspective of children's dependency, vulnerability, and needs. This seems to contradict the agentic child discourse of the 'new sociology of childhood'. Neale and Smart (1998) argue that understanding the role of both (agency and dependency) perspectives is important for progress in children's rights and the extent to which their potential for agency is recognized and permitted to flourish:

> The dependency paradigm does not have taken for-granted status but it is not dismissed. It is acknowledged in order to explore how children themselves experience it in relation to their agentic selves, how their self defined rights to participate fit in with their self defined rights to protection and care, how their rights to autonomy fit in with their basic rights (under the UN Convention) to integration within a caring family. This approach allows, then, for the individualised ethics of justice, independence and autonomy to be seen alongside the more interdependent ethics of responsibilities, relationships and care.
>
> (Neale and Smart, 1998: 15)

Second, in attempting to create a framework of rights that applies in all contexts, the UCNRC is innately universalist and has been criticized for representing a dominant, western perspective of childhood (Burr, 2004). Third, assumptions about 'a child's best interests' are often framed by adults' perspectives (Jones, 2011) and are no nearer to respecting children's agency (and rights) than dependency presumptions about their needs. Fourth, even when studies found methods to demonstrate children's capability to make decisions about their lives and to exercise their agency (e.g. Alderson, 2003; Clark and Moss, 2008; Clark et al., 2005), they are nonetheless situated and so constrained within a world that is dominated by adults' views, beliefs, and power. Finally, rights are often associated with responsibilities and this is problematic where babies and very young children are concerned (MacNaughton and Smith, 2009). As Burman has argued about the UNCRC, 'irrespective of its laudable aims, its principles still require translation or interpretation into specific cultural practices, and therefore offers scope for the maintenance of some of the same sets of abuses it was formulated to eradicate' (Burman, 2001:10).

Furthermore, despite serious attempts to find multiple ways to 'listen to young children' and recognize their rights and agency, the involvement of babies and children under 2 years in any reported public/civic decision-making (including systematic and formal decision-making within daycare settings) is rare when compared with the participation of children aged 7 or above (Graham-Matheson et al., 2009), although the latter is far from widespread in itself. Nevertheless, we have tried to show in Chapter 8 how two babies demonstrated their views and how Leila unknowingly exerted her agency to effect change when she cried (and cried and cried) herself to sleep.

There have been calls to reject dualistic arguments within the field of children's participation as an area for study and practice. At a gathering of international scholars in 2008, their discussions led to 'criticism of (false) dichotomies, e.g. adult rights vs. children's rights; individual rights vs. collective rights; dependent vs. independent participation; decision-making in family vs. public sphere' (ESF, 2008: 7–8).

In 2012, Penelope Leach highlighted the very specific issue of babies' rights in response to the NPSCC's report on the abuse and neglect of babies under 1 year old. Referring to the articles of the UNCRC, she posited that:

> The CRC makes it very clear that from the moment of birth children's individual rights must be recognised and protected, even though those rights may clash with their parents' wishes. How easily and how well parents exercise their child's rights on her behalf partly depends on the extent to which they are and have been able to exercise their own human rights.
>
> (Leach, 2012: 7)

In emphasizing the interconnectedness of rights, Leach touches on an area of the UNCRC that has drawn further criticism: its focus on children as individuals with rights related to their perception as such, which contradicts collectively oriented cultural perceptions of children as part of families within which the rights of the family as a whole supersede those of individual members (Burr, 2004). But attempting again to bridge the divide, Kjørholt (2011) suggests that sensitivity to local, cultural beliefs and practices means that respect for the views and rights of young children need not necessarily mean a lack of respect for others, including the families and communities to which they feel they belong.

Despite difficulties and disagreements that have been associated with different perspectives about what a child or childhood is, Neal and Smart (1998) have suggested that children's ontological status (what it is to be a child) could be transformed if listening to children's views became the norm. But listening is just the first step in a process that seeks to redress inequalities in power distribution (Clark et al., 2005). This demands not only a shift in attitudes for some (that children, including babies, are worth listening to, capable of expressing their views, and have something valuable to say) but also for finding ways and making efforts to listen to, understand, and respond to the different ways that babies, indeed all people, express themselves; or what Loris Malaguzzi called 'The Hundred Languages of Children' (Edwards et al., 1998: 3).

> Regardless of whether children are thought to have innate rights (as autonomous beings) or have to be granted these rights (as depend-ants), they need to define and operationalise their own rights (as active agents of their lives). According to this formulation, children's rights to be listened to are self determining and socially contextualised, arising out of and in tune with their own lived experiences.
>
> (Neale and Smart, 1998: 16).

What is childhood for?

In 2006, Martin Woodhead was commissioned to prepare a background paper for the United Nations Educational, Scientific and Cultural Organization's (UNESCO) Education for All Global Monitoring Report. In that paper he too cites the developmental, socio-cultural, and human rights paradigms as perspectives that have been three of the most influential in shaping early childhood policies and practices.

1   A developmental perspective emphasizes regularities in young children's physical and psychosocial growth during early child-hood, as well as their dependencies and vulnerabilities during this formative, phase of their lives.
2   A political and economic perspective is informed by develop-mental principles, translated into social and educational interven-tions, and underpinned by economic models of human capital.
3   A social and cultural perspective draws attention to respects in which early childhood is a constructed status and to the diversi-ties of ways it is understood and practised, for, with and by young children, with implications for how goals, models and standards are defined, and by whom.
4   A human rights perspective reframes conventional approaches to theory, research policy and practice in ways that fully respect young children's dignity, their entitlements and their capacities to contribute to their own development and to the development of services.

(UNESCO, 2007: 4).

The extent to which one or more of these perspectives is exercised reflects how a society, culture or group's dominant ideology and priorities conceptualizes what childhood is and is for. The dominance of a political and economic view may be evidenced by an instrumental or utilitarian understanding, whereby childhood serves a purpose above and beyond the individualistic, developmental perspective from which it is purportedly derived and on which it relies. Childhood becomes more than a preparatory phase in a person's journey towards adulthood; it may serve as the bedrock of future performance: the starting point on a journey towards fulfilling one's potential as a contributor to the economic and political wellbeing of the nation where 'inputs' invested during early childhood will later be rewarded through the 'outputs' of the adult he or she becomes.

An alternative view is one that sees children and childhood as an asset in its own right, including economically, without recourse to calculations of 'pay-back' at a later date exceeding initial costs or 'outlay' whether that is financially, emotionally or practically.

Based on his work for a similarly internationally focused report on ECEC in 20 countries for the (OECD 2006), Bennett advises that,

> All individuals have multiple identities and qualities that cannot be captured by broad labels. Each child is talented and competent in his or her own way, and when born into adverse backgrounds can show extraordinary inner strength and resilience. Successful programmes do not categorise young children as having developmental or language needs, but believe that young children will learn and develop quickly if given a supportive, pedagogical environment. The inclusion of these children in universal programmes seems the most acceptable and effective approach.
>
> (Bennett, 2006: 150)

Sadly, however, the broader policy frameworks within which 'these children' are identified demonstrate a deficit, compensatory paradigm that labels the children even if the successful programmes (or settings) do not do so themselves. In these frameworks, the childhoods of 'these children' are seen to be in need of greater intervention in the early years to make up for what is perceived to be otherwise lacking and to prevent a failure to fulfil one's potential (whatever that means). This is particularly evident where early childhood is deemed to be a preparation for compulsory schooling. In his earlier reflections on the first OECD report, *Starting Strong* (OECD, 2001), Bennett noted that,

> All societies have a project for young children, and an attempt to ensure a fair start in education for all children is a worthy aim. As in many matters, it is fundamentally a question of choice and balance.

However, in the desire to provide compensatory cognitive environments for young children from disadvantaged backgrounds, broader
aspects of the learning process may be overlooked, and care and
social support neglected.

(Bennett, 2003: 32)

Having analysed the curricular approaches of ECEC in the 20 participating
OECD countries, Bennett suggested that they fell into two categories: the pre-
primary tradition and the social pedagogy tradition – the former focusing on
cognitive and behavioural skills and the latter 'the whole child, the child with
body, mind, emotions, creativity, history and social identity' (Bennett, 2005:
18). He suggests that the pre-primary tradition employed a greater focus on
cognitive skills and within a wider framework of cognitive compensation and
narrowly defined school readiness a worry must be that care and social support
will slip further down the list of priorities.

Discursive constructs of babies and daycare
provision for them

'Seven right, yes. Six left, yes!' he whispered. 'This is it. This is the
way to the back-door, yes. Here's the passage!' He peered in, and
shrank back. 'But we durstn't go in, precious, no we durstn't.
Goblinses down there. Lots of goblinses. We smell them. Ssss! What
shall we do? Curse them and crush them! We must wait here, precious,
wait a bit and see.'

(Tolkien, 2009: 111)

What has felt like a long introduction to the specific discourses of babies'
education and care has merely been a quick helicopter flight skimming its
surface. It has allowed us to look down on major rivers running through an
Amazonian jungle of paradigmatic debates in which myriad tributaries and
streams flow into, across, and away from one another. So far, we have mainly
referred to 'the child' or (early) childhood and now wish to focus more closely
on babies.

It is easy to see how babies have not fared well in the major paradigms that
shape attitudes about who they are and what they need, deserve or tell us they
want. Naive interpretations of developmental perspectives have construed
them as the least 'formed'; in economic terms as the most 'costly'; in socio-
cultural terms the most 'inscrutable'; and in rights-based discourses they are
virtually 'invisible' with the exception of (some) attention to others' perceptions of their best interests, rather than any they might self-determine or
articulate.

As the participants in the project described their work with babies, they often described them as parents' 'most precious thing(s)'. Sometimes this was accompanied by disbelief, concern or even anger that a parent would 'choose to leave' their baby for hours in daycare; sometimes with empathy and sympathy for the emotional outpourings they witnessed from parents and babies who experienced a trauma of separation, particularly for the first time. In describing the preciousness of babies, they were implicitly revealing a discourse of relationships, ties, and belonging. Despite the possibilty of interpreting this discourse as including a sense of ownership, the babies' worth did not lie in their economic value or potential, but seemed to be a reflection of the love and care that these practitioners attributed to the parents' relationship with their babies.

We asked them to reflect on their roles in response to being asked, 'Who do you think you are?' We gave them two further prompts: 'Who are you at work? How would (or do) you describe yourself to other people?' This was a three-step process involving initial, independent ideas; then group discussion; then categorization of the groups' ideas. They brought their ideas together and agreed on 'being' and 'doing' categories. Their individual responses are shown in the cloud tag in Figure 7.1, which enlarges the size of words the more frequently they were used.

The participants' individual responses included a combination of dispositions, traits – 'unconscious behavioural habits' (Colker, 2008: 2) – and skills (or activities that suggested particular skills). Many of the descriptions they associated with their roles once again reflected a pedagogy that focused on caring relationships, with the babies, their colleagues, and with parents. There was a noticeable absence of any overt descriptions concerned with developing, learning, teaching, educating with the exception perhaps, more implicitly, of role model, although this pertained not to the relationship with babies but with less experienced members of the baby room team. Jean Rockel (2009: 2) has argued that in New Zealand a push for 100 per cent qualified (as teacher) staff for ECEC for infants and toddlers, combined with the Te Whāriki

Figure 7.1   Practitioners' individual responses to being asked 'Who do you think you are?'

curriculum has helped to bring about a shift in the concept of care. She says that it has evolved from being conceptualized as 'watching over children who are away from their parents . . . as necessary for children's satisfactory growth and development', to being understood as 'the need to look more closely at the individual ways infants and toddlers express their desire for responsive care; and the adult's responsibilities in this process'. In the New Zealand context, she suggests that teachers who are working within an education framework need to articulate a pedagogy of care.

In the baby rooms in which our participants worked, there were no qualified teachers and rarely any input from staff qualified to degree level, let alone early years professionals whose status has been equated to that of teacher. The baby rooms are subject to the requirements of the EYFS, which set out the learning and welfare requirements for babies; its provenance is the Department for Education and practice is assessed and provision regulated by the Ofsted. Therefore, the participants' work falls within an education framework and yet their discursive constructs of their own roles and responsibilities fall firmly within the caring domain. In New Zealand, Rockel adds, professionals have been challenged to respect babies' agency and to work with 'the notion of care beyond the margins of minding children and managing care within prescribed care regimes'. She says, 'Such regimes are often based on predetermined group routines; for example, children's sleep, mealtimes and toileting practices. The reconceptualisation of care within an educational framework creates a tension in continuing these regimes' (Rockel, 2009: 2). Routines were very familiar to us, having been cited in each participant's 'Day in the Life' account and being some-thing we witnessed regularly in the baby rooms.

Yet somehow there was so much more to the 'care' that the participants described and that we saw and heard than simply 'minding the baby'. There was much to suggest that the participants took great pains to respond to the babies' agency, where they recognized this and were physically able to do so. They regularly spoke of the 'babies' best interests' and their restricted attempts to fulfil these within the constraints they experienced through the perceived intrusion of more powerful voices. But this was neither a straightforward discourse of babies' needs (as perceived by them and other adults) nor a clear statement about babies' rights as agentic, self-determining people.

The complex picture we built over time and through ongoing dialogue and observations revealed the many different influences and constraints on the participants' beliefs about themselves and their roles (Powell and Goouch, 2012). They were physically and metaphorically dislocated from other parts of the settings in which they worked and the EYFS felt remote (and sometimes incomprehensible) to them. But they were also aware of the public discourses of inadequacy that circled their everyday working lives and any sense of profes-sionalism (see Chapter 3). In spite of the discourse of 'minding babies' that was endemic outside the baby rooms, within their spaces and in the project group, with encouragement they articulated the seriousness of their work, the enormity of their responsibilities, their dedication to the babies, and voiced a selflessness that motivated them to continue to work long hours for little pay or gratitude.

The value of caring

Caring has been a much maligned term and 'caregiver' positioned as the poor relation of practitioner, teacher, educator, key person, mother or primary carer. It has become a de-professionalized term, if indeed it ever was professionalized.

The policy context in Britain has encouraged women's paid employment and set care provision up as a necessity rather than a choice. The increased need has led to the creation of an occupational category of paid care or caring work. Associations with discourses of maternalism have positioned the occupation as one that demands 'natural' female or feminized qualities. Concerns about infants' and young children's attachments to mother replacements have idealized care as more than simply minding or tending and created the concept of emotional labour (Lewis, 2009). The complexity of this role has been discussed in Chapter 4 with respect to the assumption that carers will invest in nurturing relationships with babies (to compensate for the absence of parents fulfilling this role).

Prior to starting the project we were made aware, anecdotally, that many of the people working in baby rooms reportedly had low aspirations. Through the course of our work with the participants we came to understand that this was not the case for this group. Given opportunities to explore and critically reflect on their roles and especially the responsibility with which they were entrusted – caring for the parents' 'most precious things' – it became apparent that they had been working to the expectations of a low aspiring political context for babies' everyday experiences, compounded by the public discourses of inadequacy. They lived up (or down) to what had been expected of them to the very best of their abilities and with great dedication and commitment.

At the end of the first phase of the project, we asked the first group of participants to write a charter for baby rooms, listing ten things they would insist upon given the opportunity to invoke these in their work. They came up with the following:

1   A professional, knowledgeable team with drive and passion.
2   Communicating – with babies using a wide range of forms of communication, including talk, eye contact, body language.
3   Play, fun interactions.
4   Building trust – with babies and parents.
5   Sensitivity to babies' personal preferences.
6   A buddy system.

7   Thoughtful use of babies' 'unique stories' – how and when (a system for recording observations).
8   Continuity of care for babies.
9   A stimulating environment – babies move, think and do.
10 Paperwork – has a useful purpose.

(First Baby Room Group, 6 July 2010)

They revealed a construct of babies as active, engaged, and engaging, each different from one another, seeking a wide range of experiences and opportunities with people they trusted. This was not a charter for 'warehousing' babies or being second best to those that others' discourses positioned as more superior to the 'lowest of the low'.

Currently in England, daycare is expensive and the cost to parents is among the highest in the world (Save the Children/Daycare Trust, 2012). By contrast, the pay of baby room staff often corresponds to the minimum wage. The discourses surrounding daycare for babies have positioned this work as low status, which is common in the early years sector (Lash and McMullen, 2008). It is constructed as requiring few or no qualifications – a job any person can do so long as she has the instincts to mother or be maternal and can organize herself to respond efficiently to the required routines of care (minding) imposed on the group. This discourse has been challenged by Cathy Nutbrown in her Independent Review of Childcare and Early Years Qualifications (Nutbrown, 2012b).

An alternative perspective for babies' care is one that recognizes the value of and in this role and its complexity both for the babies and those who work with them. The participants in the project leapt at the opportunity to live up to the very highest expectations without sacrificing 'care' as the principal descriptor for their work. They showed how this term could represent a rich and responsive pedagogy without overt reference to 'teaching' or 'education', which were terms that they associated with other people's identities. The participants could be said to be working in their baby rooms within a 'gift paradigm'. This is a cooperative and respectful paradigm in which 'Unilateral egalitarian gift-giving establishes bonds of community between the giver and receiver by which each can recognise the existence and importance of the other' (Vaughan and Estola, 2008: 26). Many of the participants were motivated by the desire to provide excellent experiences for the babies in their care, and together they joked, 'I'm certainly not in it for the money or an easy life'. Sadly, this concept of gift-giving is overpowered by the 'exchange paradigm' that dominates the ECEC sector and reduces their work, and babies with it, to a commodity and the least significant of all the phases of education and learning as they are presently structured from cradle to grave.

8   Ecological contexts of influence

> Plaintiff and defendant! The Court has listened to your case and has come to no decision as to who the real mother of this child is. I as Judge have the duty of choosing a mother for the child. I'll make a test. Shauvna, get a piece of chalk and draw a circle on the floor. Now place the child in the centre. Plaintiff and defendant, stand near the circle, both of you. Now each of you take the child by a hand. The true mother is she who has the strength to pull the child out of the circle, towards herself.
>
> (Brecht, 1996: 94)

What shapes the experience of a baby in different contexts and over time? How do these factors and the baby's experiences relate to her development? In this chapter, we use a theoretical model to explore and try to explain two babies' observed experiences and suggest how a critical ecology could encourage exploration, reflection, and dialogue within the baby room.

We begin this chapter by describing the background to the theory that we have employed critically; explain our reasons for its choice; highlight some problems and criticisms of the theory and its application; and then use the theory as a basis for thinking about the two babies' experiences as we observed and interpreted them.

The baby in the circle

It is now commonly assumed that there is an inter-play between the environment and a person's development, although interpretations of this relationship vary. The EYFS has four guiding principles, one of which is that 'children learn and develop well in *enabling environments*' (DfE, 2012: 4; original emphasis). The view of the European Commission is that,

The pre-primary age is an especially sensitive period in children's development. A range of socioeconomic factors can have a significant negative impact on children's psychological development and chances of success at school. These include: poverty; belonging to disadvantaged social classes; functional illiteracy and low levels of educational attainment of parents; and religious traditions associated with a cultural life where literacy is not highly regarded. Although low income or ethnic minority status alone may not be a decisive factor in development, it is the *combination* of factors that leads to serious consequences for child development.

(EACEA, 2009, 11; emphasis added)

In Australia, Fleer has proposed that certain assumptions about children's development become taken for granted. She argues not only that a child's environment matters, but while it is helpful to consider socio-cultural factors, an acritical analysis will fail to recognize how socio-cultural norms limit conceptualizations and marginalize some children. From a cultural-historical perspective, she suggests that: 'development should not be located within the individual; should be viewed intergenerationally; should be thought of as part of lived everyday experience in which children are socially primed to engage; and should be dialectical in nature' (Fleer, 2005: 7).

On a different continent, the utility as well as the effects of environments has also been highlighted in a recent Action Plan for Shanghai in China, which states:

[When] kindergarten and nursery resources [are] temporarily laid aside in the adjustment of the layout, the transformation must be strictly controlled in terms of operational exploitation, and they shall be firstly used as the activity bases for children under the age of 3 or activity grounds for pre-school children in their locality. Kindergartens . . . shall be encouraged to explore education in [a] small class style and study the optimum allocation and effective use of education resources, in preparation for the coming baby booms.

(Shanghai Municipal Government, 2007: 4)

The important role of ECEC (and other) environmental features is widely accepted. Yet until the latter part of the twentieth century, studies of development were typified by:

- The removal of a baby from her 'natural' environment in studies of behaviour (and assumptions that this would be the same in any context), with the exception of anthropological studies such as Margaret Mead's ground-breaking and now legendary (and controversial) research in Samoa and New Guinea in the 1920s.

- The failure to acknowledge the ways that environments, including people in them, can influence behaviour and development and vice versa.
- The distinction between nature (heredity or genes) and nurture as separate and distinct causal factors in a baby's development.
- The tendency to focus on one aspect of a baby's development or behaviours (for example, cognition).

The dominance of 'laboratory' psychology as a basis for informing ideas and decisions about children's development and early education in the twentieth century is well documented. From the 1960s, some unorthodox psychologists began to work against the tide of the time with attempts to work in more naturalistic settings to study the psychology of children's development. John and Elizabeth Newson (Newson and Newson, 1963, 1968, 1976, 1977) became notable pioneers of a social ecology perspective when they carried out 'the most detailed and discussed British ethnographic study of childhood through parents' eyes, which spanned more than 20 years. Their work not only informed three generations of childcare practitioners about the diversity of parenting experiences, but also called mainstream psychology to account' (Lewis, 2010).

From 1979, an orientation towards a new 'ecological' perspective gained ground, although not without some resistance. Whereas the term ecological usually connoted the natural environments of plants and animals, 'Human ecology involves the biological, psychological, social and cultural contexts in which a developing person interacts and the consequent processes (for example, perception, learning, behavior) that develop over time' (Berns, 2012: 6).

The ecological systems theories of American developmental psychologist, Urie Bronfenbrenner, are credited with having had an enormous impact on how children's development and socialization are studied. His theories were not specifically concerned with ECEC and their applicability to this field has been questioned (Puroila and Karila, 2001, cited in Härkönen, 2007). Nevertheless, beyond academia his propositions and conceptual models – or elements of these – can be traced directly (through his role in the design of the Head Start Project in the USA) and more indirectly to the practices of ECEC: 'Some of Bronfenbrenner's "hypotheses" are clearly exemplified in the good practice of many schools and settings' (Brooker, 2008: 21).

While Bronfenbrenner's work is often highly praised, it has also had its share of criticisms as have some of its applications. For example, one of his former students, Nancy Darling, laments the reduction of his complex theories to simplistic and inaccurate diagrams. She writes:

> Flip open almost any introductory textbook on child development and you will find a figure in which the individual – almost always a

toddler – is seen at the center of a series of concentric circles . . . It is a busy and complex world with a passive (and isolated) child at the center.

(Darling, 2007: 204)

Interactionist ideas about child development, which Bronfenbrenner advocated, bring together the dichotomous concepts of nature and nurture. These are not without challenge (see Richards, 1998), together with the traditionally positivist paradigm within which Bronfenbrenner operated. However, it has been claimed that his relational and dynamic theory is a 'postmodern rejection of Cartesian dualities' such as nature and nurture (Jelicic et al., 2007: 439).

Penn has suggested that 'his theory was too wide and operated at too many levels to be testable' (Penn, 2008: 46), and that his concept of nested structures is 'schematized and orderly' and so unrepresentative of the complexity of life (p. 48). But perhaps the most notable critic was Bronfenbrenner himself, who spent many years highlighting weaknesses and 're-assessing, revising, extending as well as regretting and even renouncing' some of his earliest conceptions (Bronfenbrenner, 1992: 187). Bronfenbrenner was quick to recognize that his call to colleagues in his field (of developmental psychology) for ecological validity had resulted in a great focus on the features of environments where development occurs to the detriment of studies in development within those environments (Lerner, 2005). Here, we explore some of the ideas that emerged through the process of Bronfenbrenner's revisions but first we briefly set out some key elements of his original theory, since these survived his revisions and remained at the core of later iterations.

At its heart, Bronfenbrenner's original theory adopted a 'process–person–context' model (PPC) and he declared that its principal scientific power lay in 'its capacity not so much to produce definitive answers as to generate new questions' (Bronfenbrenner, 2005: 119). It is partly this spirit of ongoing enquiry that has attracted us to its adoption for a critical ecological analysis of babies' experiences and baby room principles and practices.

The PPC differed from other approaches to the study of human/child development, in that it considered all three elements of the model as essential components of research designs; it did not explore isolated domains (such as cognition); it did not separate biological and social factors from environments in exploring development; and it sought to explain *how* development occurs and constitutes a determinant of future development of the individual.

Perhaps the most commonly recognized and the analogy most often used to describe Bronfenbrenner's original Ecological Systems Theory is one in which the 'ecological environment is conceived as a set of nested structures, each inside the next like a set of Russian dolls' (Bronfenbrenner, 1979: 3). It is extremely difficult to construct a diagram to represent the fullness of his theory but the nested structures system has been widely applied in the conceptual frameworks of many studies in different academic disciplines. For example, when Maria Evangelou and colleagues carried out a literature review for the British government about learning and development of babies and children from birth to 5 years, they claimed that this concept was at the heart of their design (Evangelou et al., 2009).

Bronfenbrenner named the different systems within his model as follows:

- The *microsystem* was seen as a context in which a developing human (who is the focus for study) is directly involved, such as her home, her daycare setting, specifically the baby room or a mother and toddler group. Consequently, a person can interact with and within several microsystems. Bronfenbrenner argued that it is in the microsystems that 'processes' are at their strongest – or most 'proximal' – and 'instigative' (see below).
- The *mesosystem* represented the relationship of interactions between different microsystems and the developing person. For example, this has often been exemplified by home–nursery relations (Brooker, 2008) but the role of this relationship in a baby's development is also implicated.
- The *exosystem* has been described by Swick and Williams (2006: 372) as the psychological, rather than the physical, systems that we inhabit beyond the microsystems. Bronfenbrenner explained that the exosystem 'comprises the linkages and processes taking place between two or more settings, at least one of which does not contain the developing person, but in which events occur that indirectly influence processes within the immediate setting in which the developing person lives' (Bronfenbrenner, 1993: 24).
- Finally, in his early iteration, Bronfenbrenner proposed that there is a *macrosystem*, which represents the values and beliefs of a culture or its sub-cultures as well as the institutions and policies that constitute social organization This permeates all the other systems so that, 'within a given culture, one school classroom looks and functions much like another . . . as if all had been constructed from the same blueprint' (Bronfenbrenner, 1978, reproduced in Bronfenbrenner, 2005: 47).

Furthermore, three important aspects of his evolving 'bioecological' model (Bronfenbrenner, 2001) emphasized the following:

1   A person's experience within an environment should be viewed equally in terms of (positive or negative) objective properties and subjective feelings and their functional relationship, which is

phenomenological.[2] Darling explains this proposition is significant 'because different environments will have different affordances and will be responded to in different ways by different individuals, experienced and objectively defined environments will not be randomly distributed with regard to the developmental processes and the individuals one observes within them. Rather, one will find ecological niches in which distinct processes and outcomes will be observed' (Darling, 2007: 204).

2   A person (a baby) is both the product of her own development and partially responsible for producing this through reciprocity with the environment involving social interaction and engagement in progressively more complex activities and tasks. The extent to which a baby is seen to be (capable of) making a contribution will depend on how infancy is understood or constructed (see Chapter 7). Here Bronfenbrenner acknowledges that he had been influenced by other 'scientists', including Lev Vygotsky and his followers, Aleksei Leont'ev, Barbara Rogoff, and James Wertsch. This vision relies on a developing baby's (and child's) strength of personal characteristics to 'set in motion, sustain, and encourage processes of interaction' with the people around them together with the nature and extent to which the environment (physical and symbolic) affords or inhibits interaction that is progressively more complex (Bronfenbrenner, 1989, reproduced in Bronfenbrenner, 2005: 97). The strength of personal characteristics includes personal qualities that elicit different responses – for example, whether a baby is considered 'good' or 'fussy'. It also includes a baby's (and child's) 'environmentally oriented orientation from birth', such as being comforted when carried, responding to – reciprocating – the sounds of a familiar voice, doing so in different contexts, and which may be shaped by a genetic predisposition to the nature of the reciprocal interactions. This refinement of his theory was concerned with the inclusion of these 'developmentally instigative characteristics' and included a child's growing sense of her own agency (Bronfenbrenner, 2005: 98–9). They led to reformulations of the definitions of micro- and macrosystems to emphasize the individual, interactive 'person' aspects of the 'process–person–context' equation.

3   Bronfenbrenner acknowledged that he had originally failed to include 'the very dimension along which development occurs – the dimension of *time*', which he introduced as a fifth system, the *chronosystem* (see Bronfenbrenner and Morris, 2006). He suggested that there had been and could be different ways of exploring time as an influential dimension but was concerned to emphasize that this meant a need to explore change and constancy in the environment and how it

interacts dynamically to effect constancy or change in the developing person (and vice versa). This suggests that studies of the long-term effects of early exposure to daycare on a child's development when they reach school-age are rendered less than valid if they fail to take into account the full process–person–context–time equation. This would involve a child's interactions with her changing environment at the different points in time when the 'measurements' of behaviours and so forth are taken. For example, how her personal characteristics interacting within the micro-, meso-, exo-, and macrosystem of her baby room when she is 18 months old are the product and determinants of her development assessed in the same way in a different time and place when she is 4½ and in the first year of school. The 'outcome' at this later time is considered to be the result of *both* sets of interactions rather than simply a product of the first.

A critical ecological perspective

Bronfenbrenner intended that his bioecological model could be used as a design frame for rigorous studies in psychology, which included many assumptions and methods most closely associated with the positivist research tradition. But we see his broad and dynamic model as offering a frame for an entirely different perspective that sits more comfortably within the post-modern family of approaches, and it is in this spirit that we have borrowed his concepts.

Not only is it difficult to encapsulate the sophistication of Bronfenbrenner's ideas within a diagram, although many have tried, it is also virtually impossible to distil more than six decades' worth of his scholarship into a summary. Consequently, in our overview we have attempted to draw attention to some of the key elements of his theory over time but we recognize that we have not captured the richness of his work. Despite this caveat, we feel that the influence of his process–person–context–time model has been substantial and it also provides a useful, more holistic basis from which to consider the contexts of influence for an active, growing baby who may spend up to 50 hours a week in a baby room.

As we discuss in Chapter 9, recognition that beliefs and practices are imbued with socio-cultural and political assumptions is a step towards identifying norms that can limit experience, subjugate certain perspectives, and favour dominant ways of being to the detriment of alternative possibilities. The breadth of perspective and dynamism of Bronfenbrenner's model(s) allows us to examine how assorted social, cultural, and political constructs interact and sometimes clash; it also provides a basis for considering the ways that these position some people as more powerful than others, which is particularly important when studying the experiences of a baby whose rights, 'needs', and views are often overlooked and by association those of the people who work in baby rooms.

We are not concerned with how babies are socialized *per se* (which was Bronfenbrenner's focus). Our interest lies first in the ways that social, political, historical, and cultural assumptions, mediated to greater or lesser degrees by the exercise of power through discourses (speech, text, signs and symbols, and actions), creates a particular kind of socialization; and second in how these ideas can be questioned, becoming a source for reconceptualizing daycare and suggesting alternative possibilities. Once exposed, these possibilities can then become the focus of dialogue and debate that enrich the theorizing of policies, provision, and practice.

Sleeping like a baby

Bronfenbrenner was interested in *how* development evolves and how it is instigated and nurtured or hampered. He was also interested in how a developmental outcome fed back into the process as a determinant that shapes a person's future development processes and outcomes. Of course he saw all of this in terms of interactions. In the vignette that follows, we use these concerns to describe and discuss a scenario that emerged from practice we encountered in one baby room.

During the course of the Baby Room Project, it became clear that sleep was a major, recurrent, and troublesome issue. Sleep is a vital ingredient for healthy development (Meggitt, 2001) and co-sleeping with his mother helps a young baby to regulate his breathing, while 'thermal synchrony' in skin-to-skin contact means that a mother's body changes temperature to warm or cool her baby when he is too cold or too hot (Sunderland, 2006: 70). We propose that a baby's patterns of sleeping and waking and the ways in which these are viewed and accommodated can be exemplified using Bronfebrenner's bioecological model.

> Leila is 11 months old and spends eight hours in the baby room, three times a week. Her parents have told the setting that they want her to learn to 'self-soothe' and that she must be put in the cot and left to cry herself to sleep. This is a source of great anxiety for the baby room staff and upsets and disrupts the other babies. During a filmed observation, Leila was duly put into the cot by her key person who then left her. Despite clear signs that she was tired and ready for a nap, Leila's cries became increasingly high pitched, seemingly indicating her soaring distress levels. Her key person returned every few minutes to peer at her through a window and check she was 'safe' and her own anxiety at this process was evident during the 45 minutes it took for Leila finally to fall into an exhausted sleep. The room supervisor

later explained how difficult this situation had been to manage since the baby room team wanted to respect the parents' wishes but also felt that method that they had dubbed 'self-soothing' was a harmful form of neglect. They subsequently decided to approach her parents to discuss alternative possibilities.

Leila's developing sleep patterns and routines were happening in at least two microsystems that we knew of: her home and the baby room. She was experiencing constancy in both microsystems in terms of the superficial, objective experiences within those settings – being left to cry herself to sleep in both places. But her subjective feelings and those of others she encountered may have differed. We do not know how her parents felt when Leila cried, though it is possible that they found it difficult despite having advocated the method. But we know that her key person felt and exhibited distress about this process as did other staff in the baby room and other babies who were present. There was discontinuity in Leila's mesosystem in relation to ideas about her sleep. Initially, in terms of the power differentials involved, it might be argued that the conflicting ideas about how Leila should self-soothe were firmly outside her control and it could be argued that it might be better reconstructed as an exosystem in which Leila had no agency. The baby room staff did not agree with or want to comply with the parents' method but felt obliged to do so. The macrosystem helps us to understand why this might have been happening: the parents had heard about (or been advised about) a 'self-soothe' method and decided to try this for themselves, presumably believing it to be appropriate and effective. This is common and many new parent self-help books and websites advocate a range of ways of 'getting your baby to sleep', from the 'leave them to cry' method at its most extreme to variants that include popping back every few minutes to reassure a baby or sitting somewhere quietly in the same room without making eye contact and waiting for the baby to go to sleep before leaving. In contrast, the practitioners were working to a very different set of beliefs. Their opinion that this approach was equivalent to neglect stemmed from their affective responses to the distress in Leila's crying, a resistance to the imposition of a procedure they did not normally employ, a belief that there was, somewhere, a 'regulation' that prohibits this behaviour in nurseries because it is 'harmful'. Their view also represented an alternative public discourse that is found in parenting books and websites and which recommends a very different approach.

Leila's lengthy period of crying was a product of her prior experience of having been rocked to sleep in her various carers' arms at home and at nursery and being faced with a change she could not control. As Small (1998: 116) observed, parents are in control and 'it is their folk wisdom that dictates sleeping arrangements', be that where, when or how this happens. Sunderland (2006: 79) has argued that 'a baby is not capable of settling himself to a state of inner peace . . . If a child feels anxious about being alone, the pituitary gland in his brain sends a hormone (ACTH) to his adrenal glands, which respond by producing the stress hormone cortisol'. In terms of how Leila's biological response might represent a determinant of her future development, Sunderland explains that a lack of response to crying simply trains a baby out of the instinct to cry and has the possible long-term effect of hypersensitivity to stress and an inability to self-soothe – precisely the opposite of the intended outcome. It is partly this discourse (of developmental risk) that supported the practitioners' perspective.

In Bronfenbrenner's terms, leaving Leila to cry does not allow her to engage in the increasingly complex biological, emotional, and social processes that he believed help her to feel that 'being settled for a nap is a safe and secure business' and to become reassured as she internalizes the concept of 'permanence' that allows the confidence to fall asleep knowing that when she wakes that she is in the same place (Robinson, 2003: 108) and it was a good place to be when she fell asleep. But Bronfenbrenner's model is also phenomenological. This means that Leila's 'reality' is the one that exists in her consciousness. What does the experience of being left to cry feel like to her, what does the world around her seem like to Leila at that time, and what is she learning from this that will influence her subjective experiences, her consciousness in the future?

Leila's agency is seemingly severely hampered in terms of a response to her plight that she sees and feels. She voices her distress but is unaware that this is reciprocated as her key person and other staff members fret about her, feel discomfort and frustration, and peer in to check on her. So, from her perspective, the resistance that she displays is not acted upon and in her phenomenological world at that time the 'locus of control' has been removed from Leila's grasp. Beyond what Leila perceives, she has in fact had a significant impact and ultimately her crying causes the practitioners to discuss with Leila's parents how things might be done differently. But in the meantime, Leila has learnt that nobody comes when she cries, whether that is in her home or in the baby room and the mesosystem – between her two miscrosystems – supports this (lack of) response.

Neglect, which was how the project participants construed the situation in which Leila was left to cry, has been shown to be much more likely for children under 12 months than for older children. In their report on neglect and abuse of babies in Britain, a team from the National Society for the Prevention of Cruelty to Children (NSPCC) used an ecological model based on Bronfenbrenner's work to highlight the causes and consequences of babies' maltreatment. Although each element of their model, reproduced in Figure 8.1, is important in its own right as a part of the ecological jigsaw puzzle, the ontogenic loop demonstrates how all aspects of the model at any one time (such as during infancy) feed back into subsequent development, whether

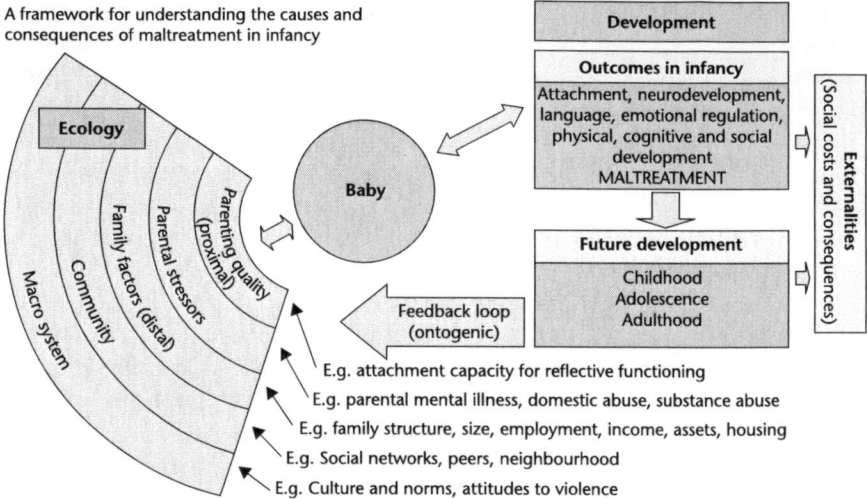

A framework for understanding the causes and consequences of maltreatment in infancy

E.g. attachment capacity for reflective functioning
E.g. parental mental illness, domestic abuse, substance abuse
E.g. family structure, size, employment, income, assets, housing
E.g. Social networks, peers, neighbourhood
E.g. Culture and norms, attitudes to violence

Figure 8.1 [Ecological] framework for understanding the causes and consequences of maltreatment in infancy.

Reproduced from Cuthbert et al. (2011: 20) *All Babies Count: Prevention and Protection for Vulnerable Babies*, with permission of the NSPCC

those are factors most closely associated with parental quality or are concerned with society's beliefs about violence towards children and how these two aspects interact with each other and the developing baby. What happens in infancy, the interaction in a baby room, is vitally important for determining *what* happens later and *how* it happens and is distinct, organic, and dynamic in every baby's case.

Where have all the good guys gone?

In contrast with a crying baby, a quiet baby, the sort who does not 'make a fuss', was highlighted when the Baby Room Project participants reviewed their own video observations. These became known to the group as 'the "good" babies', an example of which forms the basis for our next vignette.

> *Tyler spends five days a week in the baby room while his Mum is at school. His Nan drops him off in the mornings and his Mum collects him in the afternoons. He lives with them both nearby and his key person knows the family well, being local herself. Tyler is 12 months old (his birthday was a few days ago) and he has been coming to the setting since he was 13 weeks*

old. During lunch today, Tyler was asleep and woke up after everyone else had finished. A little bleary eyed, he is brought to a low table and placed on a little chair by a member of staff (not his key person). He sits still and speechless as he is given a plate of finger food including breadsticks, carrot pieces and sliced grapes. 'Are you hungry Tyler? Here you are, do you want to eat your dinner?' He is given a beaker of water and left to his own devices while the two members of staff busy themselves with four other babies who are playing in the room. Tyler sits and watches the other babies for a while and then looks at his food. Slowly and seemingly a little half-heartedly he fingers the food and then begins to nibble a breadstick with his gaze fixed in front and away from the small group of staff and babies. He continues to eat his food, slowly and methodically and occasionally drinks from his beaker. He makes no sound but the room is filled with the noises of the other babies and the staff as they talk and play. After 15 minutes, a member of staff comes to check on Tyler and to comment on what he has and has not eaten.

(From a filmed observation in a baby room, September 2011)

Tyler's isolation in this example is palpable and yet he does not protest or indicate that he wants or expects company while he eats. He is – or has become – one of 'the "good" babies' who easily disappear from mind because they seldom demand attention. It could be argued that Tyler might previously have indicated that this is his preference and that he enjoys the solitude but the participants' reflections on the video revealed this was not the case. We also would need to ask why he might have such a preference if that had been shown to be the case. He had simply been overlooked because he was quiet. Equally, dominant macrosystemic values could have influenced the silence he endured as he ate his lunch. We had often witnessed snack and mealtimes where the familiar phrase, 'don't talk with your mouth full' was heard. Yet this countered the culturally imbued philosophy that mealtimes present prime opportunities for enjoying and learning in the company of others (Manning-Morton and Thorp, 2003) or that they provide the potential for *developmentally instigative* social interactions through which babies and children come to understand and use what Rogoff (1990) calls the tools of culture through Bronfenbrenner's concept of opportunities for increasingly complex and *reciprocal* activities (Process). In this instance, Tyler's opportunities for reciprocity seemed primarily to be with his physical environment while he sat on the periphery of human interactions from which he was excluded. Returning to the phenomenology of this event for Tyler, we wonder what he is learning about his culture through this microsystem if he experiences prolonged exposure to isolation and lack of communication and more directly about what mealtimes are like and are for, and how he perceives himself and his relationship with the other people in the baby room? This leads us to consider what assumptions underpinned the decision that Tyler should eat at this time and in this way. Who has the power to make these decisions and if they remain unchallenged, why might this be? Do alternatives provide possibilities that are 'better', and if so, on what assumptions are these based, how are they justified, who benefits and does not, how and why? In part, our approach was informed by Fairclough's suggestion that,

> We may . . . construe (represent, imagine) the social world in particular ways, but whether our representations or construal have the effect of changing its construction depends on various contextual factors, including the way social reality already is [or is perceived], who is construing it, and so forth . . . representations of aspects of the world . . . can be shown to contribute to establishing and maintaining relations of power, domination and exploitation – primarily because such representations can be enacted in ways of interacting socially and inculcated in ways of being in people's identities.
>
> (Fairclough, 2011: 123)

In this chapter, we have begun to explain how we deconstructed some of the practices that we observed, in dialogue with the participants of the Baby Room Project and what messages or issues emerged for discussion in the development session groups. Together, we challenged ourselves to expose and reconsider some taken-for-granted beliefs and practices, to explore what theories or assumptions might underpin these, to think about how power is exercised to sustain or reject them, to propose alternative possibilities and, if accepted, contemplate how these might be realized.

9   Baby rooms as contexts for democracy

> Practitioners do not confront policy texts as naïve readers, they come with histories, with experience, with values and purposes of their own, they have vested interests in the meaning of policy. Policy will be interpreted differently as the histories, experiences, values, purposes and interests which make up any arena differ. The simple point is that policy writers cannot control the meanings of their texts.
>
> (Bowe and Ball, 1992: 22)

The mention of policy often elicits groans, glazed eyes or worried expressions. It can seem remote – the preserve of a distant élite of faceless bureaucrats or glib politicians who seek our votes with promises of better times ahead. In 2006, we were responsible for organizing a conference entitled 'Make Policy Make Sense', a title that was deliberately punctuation-free to entice our delegates into a dialogue around its interpretation. For us, it represented an inextricable and dynamic relationship of policy with practice: we aimed to suggest that everyone has a role in making policy through its everyday lived enactment and that dialogue (in this case in the context of a conference) is vital if we are to make sense of policy in and for our professional lives.

It is not our intention to review successive governments' family policies or those for ECEC in the countries of the UK or across international contexts (but for those interested, see OECD, 2012; UNESCO, 2007; UNICEF, 2008). However, our experiences of their interpretations have informed this chapter.

As we explore our relationship with policies, it is important to explain what this term means to us now and how we approach the concept of policy before we begin to explore a process for making policy make sense in baby rooms from where one of our project participants observed,

> Do we need half of the policies we have? And who are some of them really serving? With a few of them, I have to ask, do we have them in

place for the good of the children, or just to tick a box when Ofsted or Early Years advisors walk through the door?

(Amy's post on the NING discussion forum in November 2011)

In the quotation from the forum on the Baby Room Project's online NING, "Amy" questioned the prudence of particular policies and indicated that she felt these were an imposition with questionable underlying purposes. Her statement reveals an expectation that a policy will have goals (which can be overt and covert), should have beneficiaries (intended and unintended), may be misguided or unnecessary, can be one of a series and come under surveillance from external parties (in this case Ofsted and early years advisors); that they may be transient or temporary, but perhaps most importantly, they are open to question and critique. Her questions for fellow project participants and their equally cynical responses also revealed disquiet with current practices, an apparent voicelessness in the development of these policies, as stated earlier, a desire to deconstruct their place in the settings and, perhaps, a search for wisdom – for finding sense in and the sense of policy and policy-making. This plea for answers from a baby room practitioner reveals her insight into many of the important issues raised in policy analyses and through their findings. These analyses have been tackled in different ways by scholars of education and social policy, and disagreements often arise about what policy is, as well as how it can or should be analysed. In this chapter, we use Amy's quotation to illustrate why policy matters and how examining policy critically is both useful for professional dialogue and essential to the development of the mindful care of babies. We will show briefly how this can be undertaken for numerous purposes in different ways and can lead to a range of insights and understandings.

So what is policy, how does it affect us, and how can we affect it?

Power relations are extremely widespread in human relationships. Now, this means not that political power is everywhere, but that there is in human relationships a whole range of power relations that may come into play among individuals, within families, in pedagogical relationships, political life and so on.

(Foucault, 1994: 283)

An investigation of definitions of the word 'policy' yields a surprising array of terms suggesting that the meaning of this little word is hard to pin down. 'Policy' appears not to have a single definition or even to constitute a straightforward concept, and has been used flexibly in practice and interpreted differently in the literature we have consulted and read. Linguistic definitions[3] include (i) a plan or course of action and (ii) prudence or wisdom.

When Levin (1997) used an analytical case study approach to describe the mechanics of government, he criticized vague academic descriptions of policy in other authors' writing. He argued that this lack of clarity inhibits our ability to recognize policy when we meet it. As we explain later, this ability to recognize policy is inherent to the capacity to position or envisage oneself as a contributor to policy production and enactment. Levin proposed that we become more alert to the characteristics commonly attributed to policy by politicians and officials – the "policy-makers" – so that we are more generally aware of policies' existence and also recognize their different facets. Therefore, he suggests that policy:

1   denotes 'belongingness' (to a particular political party, for example);
2   denotes 'a commitment on the part of those to whom a policy belongs';
3   equates a higher status with a proposed course of action and 'may constitute an attempt to get other people to accept it and to concede that it has a strong claim upon resources' and
4   will have some 'degree of specificity for it to be distinguishable from other policies'.

(Levin, 1997: 19)

We might equally argue the importance of being alert to common characteristics of policies in their use and definition in ECEC settings and we will return to this later. Meanwhile, Levin's list of characteristics might suggest that policy is simply a product of policy-makers (whether these people are officials of government or professionals working within a particular organization). However, he goes on to explain that he also sees policy as 'a selective response to interests; the outcome of a process or a reflection of the "power structure" ' (Levin, 1997: 65). Analysis of these features can help to identify the formal and informal mechanisms that bring policy to life and sustain it. Levin's ideas provide a useful framework for understanding policy and all his ideas correspond with one or more characteristics to which other scholars have drawn attention. For example, 'belongingness' reminds us of notions of democratic participation and the inclusive or exclusive domains of policy contexts of influence and production of certain individuals or groups; 'commitment' denotes particular social motives, priorities, and goals and reminds us that a demonstrable lack of commitment is an equally important 'sign of the times'; the status of policy and attempts to get others to accept it draw our attention to the power of discourse, dominant ideologies or hegemonic beliefs and practices; and the specificity of policy reminds us that no policy exists in isolation from other policies, from politics or from the 'bigger picture' of the social, cultural, and historical contexts from which it emerges. We will illustrate each of these ideas by drawing on the work of many eminent scholars of early childhood, social policy, education, and political science as we offer a tentative response to the questions:

1   What does policy reflect?
2   What is policy for?
3   And what is our relationship to policy?

Policy drivers and motives

Policies are steeped in and reflect a collective history at a particular point in time and place. Pugh's (2010) overview of a developing policy agenda for early childhood services since the 1980s in the UK begins with a short history of nursery education and childcare provision. She notes that a lack of appropriate provision within the education system for young children was an important legacy for understanding early years policy as it began to gain prominence and momentum in political circles at the end of the twentieth century.

She goes on to argue that until very recently, 'there was a lack of political conviction that young children mattered and a view that children were the private responsibility of their parents' (Pugh, 2010: 8). This resonates with the view of Daniel and Ivatts (1998: 146), who explain how social policies relating to children have been dependent on different views about children and childhood in society. They describe thematically in their book the ways that (particular views about) children are instrumental in social policy development, and that a deficit view of young children as 'not yet old enough' implicit in the use of terms such as 'under five' or 'pre-school' compounded a lack of political or policy interest. It becomes clear to see, then, how the title of the first national framework to support children in their earliest years, *Birth to Three Matters* (DfES, 2002), was an intentional political statement by its creators (led by Professor Lesley Abbott) about the value ascribed to early childhood as a socio-cultural construct and a period in and of its own right.

Yet the legacy that Pugh described, which has been typified by an education/childcare divide at a conceptual level if not a structural one (Kaga et al., 2010), has combined with deficit constructs of early childhood. Together the effect is that the value and place of young children are even more conspicuously absent where babies are concerned. The carefully selected words for the title of *Birth to Three Matters* not only emphasized the importance of this period in and of itself, but also attempted to signal a move away from a deficit view so often evidenced in the use of the words nought or zero to signify the beginning of a person's life outside the womb. The symbolic power of language to convey particular ideas and attitudes is central to policy analysis and interpretation. As suggested elsewhere (David and Powell, 2005: 244), 'it helps to consider ideas about the cultural constructions of early childhood – what different cultural groups assume about children and their place in society, and how they try to shape them as citizens'.

What is our relationship to policy?

The language(s) of policy has been described as more than that which is written in a text, although such texts have themselves been subject to differentiation as either 'readerly' or 'writerly' (Barthes, 1981) and enabling, coercive or puni- tive (Lewis, 2009). The following description of policy texts helps to illustrate how particular forms of language can be employed to restrict or invite a read- er's interaction with the policy and how it might therefore be interpreted as more or less enabling, coercive or punitive:

> A readerly policy text, therefore, would be one containing clear and unambiguous directives which are not open to question. A writerly text, in contrast, involves the reader as co-producer, co-author, as a creative interpreter of the text. The writerly text is less predictable and it does not attempt to control the reader . . . The authority derives not from the author but rather from the readers, through their quest for meaningful interpretations that suit their particular experiences and contexts.
>
> (Hall, 2001: 155)

In 2011, the British government began to revise the statutory framework for the early years (DCSF, 2008), following recommendations from a review by Tickell (2011). A revised framework was drafted and published by the Department for Education (DfE, 2012) and then subject to a period of public consultation and feedback. During one of the Baby Room Project's develop- ment sessions, the participants were invited to read and comment on the text. Their feedback was collated into a formal response, which was submitted to the DfE. It could be argued that this process of text production, opened up to public involvement, rendered the draft framework into a form of 'writerly' text. Yet our participants concurred that they would not normally have been aware of the possibility of engaging in this process, have thought to do so or been enabled to do so without being prompted and enabled through the project. Not only did they alert us to issues of opportunity and accessibility, but also to the possibility that beliefs about participatory rights and responsi- bilities precede any considerations of engagement with policy. These practi- tioners had not previously been given to believe that they had a right to comment on policy or a responsibility to use their specific and specialized knowledge and experience within baby rooms to inform policy (re)production. Democratic participation in this way was simply beyond the realm of their everyday practice but more importantly did not feature in their perceptions of their personal or professional rights, roles or responsibilities. In such instances, the writerly-ness of a policy becomes irrelevant and all policies effectively become readerly diktats.

Simpson and Connor (2011) have argued that all citizens have a part to play in taking a more discriminatory and critical attitude towards the influence of policy in our lives and the lives of those with whom we live and work. Their particular interest is in 'the everyday concerns of those who work in social care and social work, health and education', which collectively they constitute as 'social welfare' work. They have asserted that, 'Policies play an important part in shaping people's lives, but [. . .] people should also play an important part in shaping policies' (Simpson and Connor, 2011: 2). They suggest that policy awareness is the first step towards policy literacy. But perhaps an awareness of one's own participatory rights is a simultaneous necessity and this seems likely to be entwined with professional self-worth and identity (see Chapter 3). Highlighting the psychology of policy-making, Levin cautions us 'when observing policy making, to pay attention to "the individual in the situation" and the possibility that the individual's behaviour has been evoked by the conjunction of his or her situation' (Levin, 1997: 64). So subjective experience as integral to policy interpretation and enactment (see later) seems to be influential in determining a person's attitude towards any role they might have in seeing 'policy literacy' (Simpson and Connor, 2011: 3) and policy itself as being their own or other people's business.

Power in the policy cycle

Power relations abound and undoubtedly play a part in shaping perceptions of (one's role in) policy creation or re-creation, which some see as distant and immutable, while others feel it to be within the sphere of their capacity and responsibility.

Closely linked to linguistic symbolism, subjective experience, and the effects of policy language (including what is not written or said in a policy) mentioned earlier, is the idea of policy as discourse. Discourse is understood and has been studied in many different ways but the interest in policy as discourse stems predominantly from structuralist and post-structuralist paradigms or ways of thinking about the world. Broadly speaking, the former suggests that a discourse is only meaningful when it is considered as a part of a bigger social structure or 'truth' about society. The latter discards the idea that society and social acts can be explained by single theories or laws and instead considers the possibility that there are many 'truths' and that these are created and sustained through discourses. For us, dominant discourses begin with a representation of the assumed and taken-for-granted norms of social worlds that are both explicit and implicit in what is envisaged, said, written, heard, and lived multi-modally, through many different sensory forms (Kress, 2012) and sustained by the exercise of power. Each of these concepts generates a multitude of associated questions and different lenses for critically examining policies.

> Judy, the manager, asked me (very politely) whether I had a mobile 'phone and explained that they aren't allowed in the nursery. I'd already noticed a sign on the wall showing that mobiles weren't allowed, similar to the ones in hospitals, and I handed mine over. I didn't ask why and she didn't explain. It was a silent transaction where we both understood the rules of engagement. She assured me it would be locked away safely in the office while I filmed my observation in the baby room and I said I had a terrible memory and would probably need reminding to pick it up . . . sure enough, I'd forgotten all about it and had to go back, with some embarrassment at having to disturb them to buzz me in again.
>
> (Field notes from nursery visit, October 2011)

A discourse is not simply about the meaning of language but also its effects and underlying beliefs or ideologies. In the extract from our field notes above, the exchange concerning a mobile phone revealed an understanding of the language itself resulting in the immediate surrender of a mobile. But it also reveals an understanding of (or assumption about) a child protection discourse that pervades ECEC practices. The discourse relies on a shared acceptance of potential dangers to children posed by 'outsiders' and recognition of who these people are; a significance attached to child protection; and the value of a social practice such as posting signs and surrendering a mobile to enable and sustain this discourse of danger, vulnerability, and mistrust. The discourse can neither exist nor be sustained without participation in social (in-)action in the form of compliance (handing over a mobile) or resistance (refusing to do so). Olssen et al. (2004, citing Fairclough, 1992) also explain how discourses are inseparable from people's lived experiences and so discourse as social practice is both a subjective response and a constituent element of subjective experience whereby people occupy and become implicated within a discourse depending on their interpretation of its signs or may reject, experience alienation or feel marginalized by such discourses. This understanding of discourse relies on two assumptions, which are articulated by Ball:

> We live and think structures rather than simply being oppressed or limited by them . . . [and] . . .

> Discourses are about what can be said, and thought but also about who can speak, when, where and with what authority. Discourses embody the meaning and propositions of words. Thus certain possibilities for thought are constructed. Words are ordered and combined in particular ways and other combinations are displaced or excluded.
>
> (Ball, 2006: 48)

So policy as text, as discourse, and as subjectively oriented social action comes into being through our interpretations and enactment whether that is a policy that is produced and sustained in a family, a community, an organization or a society.

At a micro level, it is common to hear that a setting or school claims to have an 'Open Door Policy', which is intended to suggest an inclusive ethos or a communicative and respectful relationship with parents and carers. But it could be argued that the very need to create and promote such a policy is indicative of a context in which either the setting believes it is 'more open' than others, that it is more open than it used to be or that this is not the norm and reveals a discourse of exclusion. Many parents argue that the open door policy is simply rhetoric – feeling the exclusionary discourse – and they do not experience the kinds of welcome the policy purports to create and describe (see, for example, Angelides et al., 2006; Heath, 1983; Moje et al., 2004; Mooney and Munton, 1998; Tveit, 2009)

> When I left James at nursery, well parents weren't allowed into the actual room where the children go. We're only allowed in the reception. James used to go straight away round to the patio door in his room because he found out that he could see me when I walked down the path and wave goodbye to me through the window. It became a little ritual. But then the manager covered the bottom half with paper so he couldn't see out any more. One day my Mum dropped James off for me and she asked why they'd done this. They told her it had been upsetting the other children so they'd covered it up and that was that. But what about James and me? It felt like we didn't matter and I felt quite upset. Their so-called 'open door' is nonsense. They made me feel really unwelcome and that I'd been doing a bad thing, but what could I do?
>
> (A parent's story, June 2011)

This parent's story demonstrates the powerlessness she felt in determining how the setting's open door policy became manifest through its interpretation and enactment. She therefore equated the policy with meaningless rhetoric: the setting did not feel open or welcoming to her, the door not only shut her out but shut out James's attempts to have some control over how they parted.

But it also reveals the complexities involved in trying to make policy that suits many within the context of potentially conflicting agendas: perhaps other children's parents had complained; the manager's explanation suggested concerns for other children's wellbeing; and the procedures employed to 'receive' children at the setting were linked to security issues.

It is difficult to think of policy, particularly national policy, without reference to power relations. The issue of power in the responses of early childhood educators to such policies has been well documented (e.g. Canella, 1997; Fenech and Sumison, 2007; Osgood, 2006), and it has been suggested that dominant discourses inherent in national policy are both oppressive and capable of facing resistance from early years workers. But such practices are also apparent in relation to the micro-politics of early childhood settings where in-house policies, such as those that caused Amy to lament on the NING, are created. What do these power relations look like and feel like? Who is directly and indirectly involved, why and with what effects?

Central to this complexity is the idea of pluralism in which a society or group comprises diversity and has a political democracy, which in theory is intended to serve different interests and lifestyles. But within a pluralist society, the power relations, such as those that Foucault describes, are often irregularly distributed within discourses that simultaneously include and exclude; in the bi-directional interactions and influences between 'state' and 'citizen' (Giddens, 1984; Stones, 2005, 2007); and in the case of the parent's story, the immediate multi-directional interactions between a parent, a practitioner and, of course, James himself together with the 'invisible scripts' that they embody (see Chapter 10). The complexity can be intensified by differences between overt and covert policy motives. Referring to the invisibility of children, particularly young children in social policy, Daniel and Ivatts (1998: 5) noted that despite a large volume of legislation that purported to be concerned with children's welfare, 'on closer inspection it becomes clear that legislation that is enacted in the name of children frequently arises out of a variety of concerns that have little to do with the needs or interests of children'. This echoes Amy's concern, which she expressed on the NING that some policies did not seem to be motivated by child-centred intentions. Despite a period since 1997 of 'particularly prolific' early years policy development (Baldock et al., 2009: 143), examples of children's invisibility can still be found in policy documentation.

Talking policy

When Olssen and colleagues examined liberal education policies from a critical perspective, they claimed that, 'the state represents *unevenly* the influence of different groups and sectors of the society ... through its official educational policy documents . . . policy is about the exercise of political power and the language that is used to legitimate that process' (Olssen et al., 2004: 71–2; original emphasis). This reveals two important distinctions, the first being that a policy represents choices made by a minority, purporting to be for many or all, but not representing the views of everyone or benefiting them; and the second being the choice of particular words to convey a policy message. In other words, 'you can please some of the people some of the time' (but who decides which people?) and you need to 'read between the lines' (because sometimes messages are multiple and the least popular or more contentious may be buried).

With the deployment of language as a device there also comes symbolism in the absence of language and in silence. What is not said in a policy may be just as important as or even more important and illuminating than what is included. The project participants were particularly vocal in their identification of the distinct lack of references to babies and toddlers in the revised draft EYFS during their response to the consultation.

A further example can be found in the first national childcare strategy for England. In 2004, the former (New Labour) government issued *Choice for Parents, the Best Start for Children: A Ten-year Strategy for Childcare* (HM Treasury, 2004). We do not believe it is naive to consider the title suggested equal measures of emphasis on 'choice for parents' and 'best start for children'. The document is ninety-one pages long and roughly four pages of the main text plus a seven-page appendix entitled 'Child Development' are directly concerned with children, although not from a child's point of view. The remaining eighty-or-so pages are dedicated to describing the mechanisms that bring about choice for parents. The following quotation illustrates the tone and perspective employed throughout the document and comes from a section about 'Childcare and very young children':

> Although the quality of the childcare experience is vital to child outcomes, there is evidence to suggest that parents do not accurately observe the quality of the childcare they use. Given that parents do not usually attend childcare settings and that the children are not old enough to give reliable comparative information, this is not surprising.
>
> (HM Treasury, 2004: 67)

The authoritative language employed leaves little room for questioning the 'wisdom' or the 'truth' of the document's claims. Aside from the various accusations levied at 'parents', the publication three years earlier and widespread acknowledgment of the 'Mosaic Approach' to listening to young children in early childhood services (Clark and Moss, 2001) makes it highly surprising to us that this attitude pervaded the document. It suggests further evidence that this policy is neither 'for' children nor even very much 'about' children in their own right. HM Treasury's role as lead author (with the Department for Education and Skills, Department for Work and Pensions, and Department for Trade and Industry) is a further clue to the policy document's underlying economic motive. One justification for particular policy motives can be the employment of evidence from research to support a particular perspective or goal (Belsky, 2009). The moral of this story seems to be: don't judge a (policy) book by its cover.

Policy goals

Just as motives or drivers for policies may be diverse or indistinct, so too can their goals or objectives, particularly as these emerge through a process of subjective interpretation. Bowe and colleagues' (1992) policy trajectory suggests three contexts for policy production, the first of which is the context of influence. At national policy level, there may be competing priorities and agendas, with departmental silos that vie for superiority within political discussion and policy development. Eisenstadt provides an insider account of the importance of the Blair–Brown (Prime Minister–Chancellor of the Exchequer) relationship in the 1990s without which, she asserts, 'there would not have been a Sure Start' in England, which epitomized a new way of devising policies and delivering services by cutting across traditional bureaucratic boundaries (Eisenstadt, 2011: 7). Nevertheless, our earlier example of the Childcare Strategy demonstrates that inter-departmental policy influence does not necessarily enable a balanced coexistence of goals or beneficiaries.

This may reflect what Ozga (2000) calls the bigger picture and why she cautions against a neglect of this landscape in attempts to analyse policies. This bigger picture concerns dominant ideologies or 'hegemony', which the revolutionary Italian political theorist, Gramsci, saw as the establishment of 'moral, political and intellectual leadership in society as a whole, thus equating one's own partisan interests with the interests of society as a whole' (Carr and Hartnett, 1996: 148). This is sometimes called a struggle for hearts and minds and refers to winning over opinions and allegiances to a particular viewpoint by a dominant minority. It neglects perspectives, interests or beliefs that may constitute alternative ideologies within the bigger picture of what Ball describes as 'what those who inhabit policy . . . do not think about' (Ball, 2006: 48). Osgood illustrates this clearly through her deconstruction of policy texts and analysis of the discourses that shape the practices of nursery workers. Her critical, feminist perspective exposes inequalities and through a classed analysis she shows how policies intended to support 'the needs of the working mother fail to incorporate the needs of the nursery worker, who might also be a mother' (Osgood, 2012: 44). Indeed, many of the participants in the Baby Room Project were mothers (and two grandmothers) and expressed anxieties around the inadequacies of their own children's care as they worked, in some cases, for 10-hour days, looking after other people's babies for a salary and with conditions that had severely restricted their own childcare choices. This brings us back to socio-cultural constructions about who and what are valued in society and how an ideology is justified and attains a dominant status.

Policies as dialogic tools and baby rooms as contexts for democracy

We began this chapter by noting that the mention of policies often elicits a negative or neutral response. But what if policies became a source of thrilling debate and intellectual challenge at the heart of every setting? More than this, as a source of challenge and democratic participation? Dahlberg and Moss (2005) have proposed that every early childhood setting is a potential site for political deliberation. They suggest that this is an ethical responsibility of everyone in the field of ECEC.

Miller and Hevey (2012: 2) have asserted that 'it is essential for all practitioners and others committed to early years services to achieve not just an awareness of policy and its implications for practice' but to become policy literate. They seek to support practitioners in understanding policies and their impact, in trying to analyse and question what policies include and leave out, and in beginning to identify underlying issues and goals. We support their aim wholeheartedly and have tried to identify some of these issues as we perceive them and as they have emerged from the Baby Room Project. We also suggest that another important step is to recognize the mechanisms that hinder or facilitate this process and find ways to increase the latter.

Our purpose in examining policy is similar to that of Ozga (2000), who took a critical perspective to educational research and described her orientation towards a 'social science "project"', which explores the relationship between practitioners and policy. Our underlying motive is a conviction that a critical exploration of this kind has inherent value as a professional development activity and can usefully contribute to the possibilities for an ever-changing series of policy–practice interactions in the field. Policy becomes social action and social action is the critically applied embodiment of policy or a means of resistance.

Perhaps this begins with an awareness of one's own and others' sense of a right to participate, of recognizing that disagreement may be at the heart of democratic participation, to have a voice and develop a vocabulary of participation, to examine critically the assumptions that normalize and subjugate and consider what is not said as well as what is, deriving dialogue from the richness of experience in practice. If practitioners seek to represent and promote babies' best interests, there is also a responsibility to enable their participation in democratic decision-making. While making assumptions about what babies' interests might be is problematic, taking them into consideration in decision-making is not and is central to decisions that emerge from warm and reliable relationships. A pedagogy of listening is essential as is recognition of the hundred languages that babies use to express themselves (Edwards et al., 1998). Just as in Reggio Emilia, where this pedagogy originates and where pedagogical documentation is a source of democratic reflection and negotiation, so too can policies (written, spoken or enacted) become dialogic tools. Consequently, awareness of the mechanisms that support or prevent participation apply equally to individual babies as to each of their carers and to them all as members of a baby room community and wider socio-cultural and political context. When decisions are (to be) made it seems politic to ask,

- Who made this decision and who was not involved?
- What has been included and what has been left out?
- What is the context for the decision?
- What motivated the decision? What are its goals?
- What are the alternatives?
- Whose interests are served and whose are disregarded? Why is this?
- What is the justification and how credible does this feel for all concerned?
- How will the outcome be better than any alternative possibilities?
- How can we continue to reflect on this decision?
- What are its effects?

It is clear then that policy is not simply a 'product' but forms a 'process' (Ozga, 2000), a 'trajectory' (Bowe et al., 1992), 'a reflection of the power structure' (Levin, 1997). It has been conceptualized not only as text, such as the UN Convention on the Rights of the Child (United Nations, 1989), but also as discourse and as social practice (Fairclough, 1992; Olssen et al., 2004).

Our assumption that possibilities for change can and do arise and we can effect such opportunities means that we do not perceive of agency as decentred in a move away from the self as subject and into questions of power/knowledge discourses (Caldwell, 2007) that disembody and so disempower the individual. Nor do we see a simplistic and separate duality of agency and structure. Instead, we insist on a belief in the exerted agency of those individuals who consciously or unconsciously make policy an everyday social practice and a co-construction that has multiple forms. But also in the latent agency of those who have yet to find a way to contribute to policy through social practice as process, product or a reflection of the power structures of which they are a part. The mechanisms that give life to and sustain policies will lead to variations in interpretation and will permit or restrict different degrees of involvement according to individuals' perceptions of their own and others' rights, responsibilities, and constraints they feel.

If we see policy as remote and the preserve of others, if, as Dean (2006) says, it is about an uneven distribution of power from the top down, then we immediately render our ability, or see our capacity to produce, reproduce or reinvent policy as entirely dependent on unequal distributions of power in which we have less agency than others higher in the policy hierarchy.

But if we see policy represented through our own and others' social actions, it becomes possible to envisage our vital contribution to all policy and policy is rendered defunct without such contributions. But if, as Foucault argues, those contributions are the subject of unseen forces, unrecognized as forms of control, then it also becomes vital to critically reflect on our social action as policy that influences not only the micro-context of a particular setting, such as a baby room, but also the much bigger and more influential contexts beyond. If we conform to and sustain a discourse of subjugation and a lack of criticality that enables recognition of the role we play in its perpetuation, then we cannot claim to reinvent policy, politics or the ideologies in which we live and work even if we believe them to be unjust.

10 Conclusion

From a double narrative to a double hermeneutic

This book has emerged from a research and development project, the Baby Room Project, which has provided us with rich stories, research narratives, new knowledge and insights and a wealth still of unanswered questions. We have endeavoured to analyse and weave themes and our learning through each of the chapters, although it is clear to us at the end of this journey that there is much for us still to learn. In this book, it has been important to separately interrogate research paradigms, policy, theoretical knowledge, and the contexts of influence that surround and underpin this field of study, although the constant binding thread throughout has been the project narratives, the participants' stories. However, we began the Baby Room Project with a mission: to find out what happens to babies in daycare and, over the course of three years, we have felt drawn along a connected path, signposted with the question, 'What do the people who work with the babies think and do?' From this a plethora of other questions emerged but at their core, and indeed at the end of this study, two themes remained constant and these were that:

- What happens to babies in daycare is inextricably bound up with how their carers are positioned socially and politically and how they perceive and enact their roles as a result of this.
- Relationships are at the heart of the issue: between babies and with their carers, between carers and parents, managers, inspectors, advisers, other professionals, policy-makers and the discourses in the public domain that surround their work. It seems to us that all of these are inseparable.

From our study, these two central themes have grown in prominence and have led us to a position of certainty that they hold the key to the development of affective daycare for babies.

'Inadequacy' and vulnerability

As we read theories about babies' development, care, learning, and education and explored the policies and provision that have been established in recent years, we were struck time and again by a combination of overt and implicit headline statements and messages about daycare, for example:

- 1 in 4 middle-class babies is in childcare despite warnings it harms children's development (Clark, 2009).
- In the 2010 UK Census, nursery nurse and childminder jobs were classified sixth of nine categories (one being highest) in the hierarchical Standard Occupational Classifications structure, which is partly derived from an assessment of 'the field of knowledge required for competent, thorough and efficient conduct of the tasks' (Office for National Statistics, 2000: 9).

Together these messages have constituted a familiar discourse of inadequacy and low esteem for the work. Without doubt, this discourse had been a component in our original motivation for designing the Baby Room Project. We had heard anecdotally, and from a range of sources, that baby room practitioners were predominantly young, inexperienced, low aspiring, and poorly qualified. This story was juxtaposed with a different discourse of vulnerability, which gave rise to the question that so often underpins media stories about daycare: 'How can it be right that babies as young as six weeks are being left for many hours in the hands of "girls" who are ill-equipped with knowledge, skills or commitment to take on such an enormous responsibility of care, let alone education?'

Collusion and manipulation

Our explorations had also included forays into the field where we had spent time in an assortment of baby rooms had indeed met some very young women charged with babies' care and who were working in relative isolation. These visits left us with many questions and with an overriding sense that there was much more to this story of "inadequacy" than met the eye and that vulnerability was a concept we could apply to the carers as well as to the babies. The discourse of inadequacy was familiar to the practitioners but their embodiment was revealed to have been employed in three quite different and contradictory ways.

First, they internalized the discourse, felt it unjust but lived with its normalizing and demeaning implications. Some of the participants' stories suggested a practice of 'docile' compliance. But they also displayed a lack of awareness of how this stance would lead to the reproduction of the very struc-tures that they claimed were unjust representations and oppressive in nature. These examples of submission appeared to conform to the invisible scripts and helped to perpetuate the regulatory practice that 'they' (seen and unseen forces) were claimed to impose upon them and which they were helpless to resist or lacked the confidence and wherewithal to reject. Freire (1970) refers to this apparent lack of awareness as 'naïve consciousness', and says it contributes to the internalization of oppressive structures, rules or discourses and thereby to a form of collusion in one's own oppression (Powell and Goouch, 2012). In many respects, this position reflects the 'Worker as Technician' whom Moss (2006: 38) describes as the embodiment of a regulatory modernity paradigm and whose practice relies on 'the possibility of an ordered world, certain, controllable and predictable, based on universal, knowable and decontextual-ised criteria and laws.'

But the Baby Room Project participants' apparent unawareness of the implications of this manifestation for them or for the babies calls into question the (intentional) 'performativity' (Ball, 2008) that is associated with the tech-nicist. Furthermore, Moss claims that these workers (whom he says are endemic within the early years and childcare workforce) value the transmission of knowledge from others to them and from themselves to babies. This was not typical of the practitioners' engagement in the development sessions of the project, although it may be of others and suggests it better reflects what is offered to them than what is valued by these practitioners.

Second, they rejected the discourse, claiming deep experiential knowledge which they further legitimized with a babies' rights perspective, albeit rhetoric at times, to support their current beliefs and practices and particularly when they felt most vulnerable themselves. This stance helped to give them the strength with which to resist the imposition of some disagreeable external demands, particularly those of parents (as demonstrated in the example of Leila's 'self-soothing').

Third, they manipulated the discourse to suit their needs, although perhaps not consciously. In this way, positioned as 'the lowest of the low' they were able to devolve themselves of responsibilities, to wrap a protective shield around themselves that excused less than exemplary practice, to rely on others' instructions and thereby shift any blame for 'inadequacy' onto the structures, processes or people surrounding them. This convenience provided a barrier to doing more than following the routines of the day. Elfer (2005: 117) has attrib-uted practitioners' immersion in the 'busyness' of their days to attempts to escape the boredom of routine and repetition that can epitomize baby room practice. An alternative explanation is that this immersion is a means of avoiding other, more challenging ways of being and to excuse this by inferring that this is what is asked or expected of them. These behaviours – minimum standards even – were adequate to fulfil the routine requirements of the day, to get by, to manage and cope with its demands, and to provide the babies with reasonable responses by drawing on reasonable resources. But is this necessary or sufficient for parents' 'most precious things?' and to sustain and retain a workforce with a characteristic warm reliability and continuity on which babies' should be able to depend?

Interpretations of practice

Taguchi (2010b: 151) has argued that 'discourse and theory have material consequences for children; for example, in the form of pedagogical practices, that is, in the ways that children are taught, related to and cared for'. Our growing understanding of the embodiment and manipulation of discourses to different effects suggested to us that Taguchi's argument was just as applicable to the practitioners as it was to the babies they cared for. The material consequence of a discourse of inadequacy is a workforce that continues to be held in low esteem despite the recent political emphasis on the importance of the early years and the neuroscience that has so influenced an agenda of 'early intervention'. Pay and conditions for baby room practitioners remain poor and rarely do those working with the babies get chosen to register for higher education courses, professional development activities or to work closely with the most highly qualified practitioners in their settings. There is little opportunity for career progression available to them and this has been directly linked to qualifications rather than experiential knowledge or unaccredited professional development. We had been told in some cases that early years inspectors, assessors or advisers rarely visited these baby rooms and when they did so these visits were characteristically fleeting and lacking knowledge or understanding of the very specialized nature of work with babies. As a consequence, some practitioners identified them with fulfilling a monitoring and surveillance activity, which offered no prospect of constructive or developmental interaction.

In 2011, the British government commissioned a review of early education and childcare qualifications. The accompanying public consultation document asked 26 questions of which the fourth was, 'There is a concern that looking after young children is perceived as "easy" work, requiring no particular skills or experience. How do you think the early childhood workforce is perceived by the general public?' (DfE, 2011). In recent years, there has been and 'continues to be significant support for early years policies and programmes' (Eisenstadt, 2011: 160), as evidenced by a succession of initiatives, not least the Sure Start programme, and independent reviews concerned with the lives, experiences, and 'life chances' of young children in Britain today (Allen, 2011; Field, 2010; Nutbrown, 2012a; Tickell, 2011, and at the time of writing a newly launched Childcare Commission). The suggestion that the public perception is of 'easy', unskilled early years and childcare work will ring true for many, not least those in the baby rooms who worked with us and for whom this negative perception was felt at its most extreme and emanated not only from the public but also, at times, from colleagues within the sector and even from colleagues working with older children within their settings. As discussed in Chapter 4, caring for babies has been construed as emotional labour and there have been calls for such work to be given due recognition and afforded a higher status than it currently enjoys. We do not disagree but would add that the intellectual endeavour of caring for babies, to meet the intense cognitive challenges of working to relational pedagogies, should also be recognized and duly acknowledged.

Developing identities for a profession

Returning to Hargreaves' contested notions of professionalism and professionalization, it is insufficient for the outsiders' view of a reconceptualized baby room worker to simply adopt constructs of an emotional and intellectual role (conduct and demeanor) in order to elevate the status of the work. The challenges extend further to include greater clarity – or at least open debate – about the aims and purposes of daycare for babies. Overtly stated, the 'grammar' of the work provides a basis for developing a sense of professional identity that accords with the grammatical rules and structure of its broader social and political frame. The current confusion caused by provision speaking to educational, economic, social care, welfare, health, and social justice aims concurrently has effectively concealed the professional vocabulary that baby room practitioners might be encouraged to learn and for it to chime with their experiences. Rather than language providing a superficial gloss of technicist responses to the regulatory gaze, it could become a source of enrichment and an essential component in the development of 'the architecture of professional selves' (Stronach et al., 2002).

Opportunities to develop the grammar of baby care resides in dialogic encounters with others who simultaneously understand, nurture, and challenge. It depends on a willingness to talk and to listen and make the investment of 'substantial selves' that Nias (1989) has proposed. This willingness to engage is a call to many: to practitioners to claim the worth of their work as intellectual, emotional, physical, social, and moral by demonstrating their commitments to each of these caring dimensions; to policy-makers to acknowledge the worth of the work, to articulate its principal aims, and to encourage and support the professional development of the workforce. Professional development is a costly business but the costs of neglecting the development of the profession are directly linked to a neglect of providing babies with 'the best start'.

State intervention in the hitherto largely private sphere of the family with regards to their children's care has increased in the last two decades. Stefansen and Skogen (2010) have suggested that in Britain, like in Norway, this intervention represents a compensatory effort and a necessary investment in future human capital to the extent that in Norway 'daycare has become the arena for informal play and peer socialization due to active state intervention in the upbringing of children' (p. 601). How would we describe the arena of daycare for babies in Britain and how might we wish to describe it? Why is there a discrepancy between these two pictures? These questions lie at the heart of our efforts to theorize baby room principles, policies, and practice.

In the Baby Room Project, we offered a platform for baby room practitioners to luxuriate in the practice of thinking about their work and from there to critically examine its inherent assumptions and implications. We became acutely aware that 'the development of how we think is affected by how we see people around us behave and how we see ourselves in their activities' (Smith, 1992: 125). The participants offered us generous insights into their worlds of work and so, through their lenses, we were allowed to see a magnified vision of their 'situated selves'. The detailed stories that emerged challenged our thinking and helped to create new possibilities for their practice. However, the question of how 'relational pedagogies' can be ensured remains, along with the problem of how the high level of 'mutual attunement' between the adults employed to care and the babies in their care can be attained. We firmly believe that the project's approach to providing relational spaces for thought and reflection and for theorizing the carers' work with babies provides a model for future professional learning. Through attendance to the situated lives of adult carers, babies' needs and rights can receive improved attention. This new, theorizing, thoughtful, attendant baby room practitioner model can only be envisioned if baby rooms become the arena for state intervention and if the corporate interests encircling the baby room business are appropriately employed, regulated, and moderated. And so, while we know that hard work needs to be done, nationally and internationally, to resolve aims and to attract investment of all kinds, ultimately we believe that progress in baby room care will be determined by the ability of each individual practitioner to become attuned to each individual baby's needs and to serve them in the best way possible. Trevarthen et al. (2003) alerts us to a lack of evidence in relation to the long-term impact of daycare on babies. Therefore, it behoves us to pay close attention to current circumstances as well as to the developing situation in local and global contexts.

When Giddens (1984) adopted the concept of a double hermeneutic for the social sciences, he believed there was a two-way relationship between a society and its studies which are 'not concerned with interpretations of things, but interpretations of interpretations' (Mantzavinos, 2009: 80). As a consequence, studies of the social world are only as rich as the interpretations on which they base themselves and the processes through which new understandings are co-constructed. Therefore, as researchers, educators, policy-makers, daycare providers, advisers or commentators, the more we can support practitioners to offer us their rich interpretations of practice, the richer our own interpretations and understandings may become. Rather than maintaining the desolate isolation of baby room practitioners, this potential synergy is surely a more sensible way to ensure that babies' care is the best our collective brains can conceive.

Notes

1. Sections from Chapter 2 have appeared in Powell, S. and Goouch, K. (2012) Whose hand rocks the cradle? Parallel discourses in the baby room. *Early Years: An International Journal of Research and Development*, and Goouch, K. and Powell, S. (2012) Orchestrating professional development for baby room practitioners: raising the stakes in new dialogic encounters, *Journal of Early Childhood Research*.
2. Phenomenology here refers to the idea that 'reality' is what is perceived in human consciousness and is not independent of this.
3. Oxford English Dictionary, Merriam-Webster Dictionary, Collins Dictionary (2012 editions).

References

Abbott, L. and Langston, A. (eds.) (2005) *Birth to Three Matters: Supporting the Framework of Effective Practice*. Maidenhead: Open University Press.

Ainsworth, M., Blehar, M., Waters, E. and Wall, S. (1978) *Patterns of Attachment*. Hillsdale, NJ: Lawrence Erlbaum.

Alderman, H. and Vegas, E. (2011) The convergence of equity and efficiency in ECD programs, in H. Alderman (ed.) *No Small Matter: The Interaction of Poverty, Shocks, and Human Capital Investments in Early Childhood Development*. Washington, DC: World Bank.

Alderson, P. (2003) *Institutional Rites and Rights: A Century of Childhood*. London: Institute of Education Press.

Alexander, R. (2008) *Essays on Pedagogy*. London: Routledge.

Allen, G. (2011) *Early Intervention: The Next Steps. An Independent Report to Her Majesty's Government*. London: Cabinet Office.

Angelides, P., Theophanous, L. and Leigh, J. (2006) Understanding teacher–parent relationships for improving pre-primary schools in Cyprus, *Educational Review*, 58 (3), 303–16.

Ariès, P. (1962) *Centuries of Childhood*. London: Jonathan Cape.

Arnett, J. (1989) Caregivers in day care centers: does training matter?, *Developmental Psychology*, 10, 541–52.

Bakhtin, M. (1981) *The Dialogic Imagination*. Austin, TX: University of Texas Press.

Baldock, P., Fitzgerald, D. and Kay, J. (2009) *Understanding Early Years Policy* (2nd edn.). London: Sage.

Ball, S.J. (2006) *Education Policy and Social Class: The Selected Works of Stephen J. Ball*. London: Routledge.

Ball, S.J. (2008) *The Education Debate*. Bristol: Policy Press.

Barnes, J., Leach, P., Sylva, K., Stein, A., Malmberg, L.-E. and the FCCC team (2006) Infant care in England: mothers' aspirations, experiences, satisfaction and caregiver relationships, *Early Child Development and Care*, 176 (5), 553–73.

Barthes, R. (1981) The death of the author, in J. Cauchie (ed.) *Theories of Authorship*. London: Routledge.

Belsky, J. (2009) *Effects of Child Care on Child Development: Give Parents Real Choice.* London: Institute for the Study of Children, Families and Social Issues, Birkbeck University of London. Available at: www.mpsv.cz/files/clanky/6640/9_Jay_Belsky_EN.pdf (accessed 10 June 2011).

Ben-Galim, D. (2011) *Making the Case for Universal Childcare.* London: Institute for Public Policy Research.

Bennett, J. (2003) Starting strong: the persistent division between care and education, *Journal of Early Childhood Research,* 1 (21), 21–48.

Bennett, J. (2005) Curriculum issues in national policy-making, *European Early Childhood Education Research Journal,* 13 (2), 5–23.

Bennett, J. (2006) New policy conclusions from starting strong II. An update on the OECD early childhood policy reviews, *European Early Childhood Education Research Journal,* 14 (2), 141–56.

Berns, R. (2012) *Child, Family, School, Community: Socialization and Support* (9th edn.). Belmont, CA: Wadsworth Publishing.

Biddulph, S. (2010) *Raising Babies: Should Under 3s Go to Nursery?* London: HarperThorsons.

Blakemore, S.J. and Frith, U. (2005) *The Learning Brain: Lessons for Education.* Oxford: Blackwell.

Blenkin, G. and Kelly, V. (2000) The concept of infancy: a case for reconstruction, *Early Years: An International Journal of Research and Development,* 20 (2), 30–8.

Bloch, M.N., Holmlund, K., Moqvist, I. and Popkewitz, T.S. (eds.) (2003) *Governing Children, Families and Education.* New York: Palgrave Macmillan.

Bowe, R. and Ball, S.J. with Gold, A. (1992) *Reforming Education and Changing Schools: Case Studies in Policy Sociology.* London: Routledge.

Bowlby, J. (1965) *Child Care and the Growth of Love* (new enlarged edition). Harmondsworth: Penguin Books.

Bowlby, J. (1969) *Attachment and Loss, Vol. 1: Attachment.* New York: Basic Books.

Brecht, B. (1996) *The Caucasian Chalk Circle* (trans. S. Brecht, 1976). Oxford: Heinemann.

British Educational Research Association (BERA) Early Years Special Interest Group (2003) *Early Years Research: Pedagogy, Curriculum and Adult Roles, Training and Professionalism.* London: BERA.

Bronfenbrenner, U. (1978) Lewinian space and ecological substance, *Journal of Social Issues,* 33 (4), 199–212.

Bronfenbrenner, U. (1979) *The Ecology of Human Development: Experiments by Nature and Design.* Cambridge, MA: Harvard University Press.

Bronfenbrenner, U. (1989) The developing ecology of human development: paradigm lost or paradigm regained, Paper presented at the *Biennial Meeting of the Society for Research in Child Development,* Kansas City, Missouri, 27–30 April.

Bronfebrenner, U. (1992) Ecological systems theory, in R. Vasta (ed.) *Six Theories of Child Development: Revised Formulations and Current Issues.* London: Jessica Kingsley.

Bronfenbrenner, U. (1993) The ecology of cognitive development: research models and fugitive findings, in R.H. Wozniak and K. Fischer (eds.) *Scientific Environments*. Hillsdale, NJ: Lawrence Erlbaum.

Bronfebrenner, U. (2001) The bioecological theory of human development, in N.J. Smelser and P.B. Baltes (eds.) *International Encyclopedia of the Social and Behavioural Sciences* (Vol. 10). New York: Elsevier.

Bronfenbrenner, U. (ed.) (2005) *Making Human Beings Human: Bioecological Perspectives on Human Development*. London: Sage.

Bronfenbrenner, U. and Morris, P. (2006) The bioecological model of human development, in R.M. Lerner and W. Damon (eds.) *Handbook of Child Psychology, Vol. 1: Theoretical Models of Human Development* (5th edn.). New York: Wiley.

Brooker, E. (2008) *Supporting Transitions in the Early Years*. Maidenhead: Open University Press.

Brooker, L. (2010) Constructing the triangle of care: power and professionalism in practitioner/parent relationships, *British Journal of Educational Studies*, 58 (2), 181–96.

Browne, N. (2004) *Gender Equity in the Early Years*. Maidenhead: Open University Press.

Bruner, J. (1986) *Actual Minds, Possible Worlds*. Cambridge, MA: Harvard University Press.

Bruner, J (2000) Foreword, in J. DeLoache and A. Gottlieb, *A World of Babies: Imagined Childcare Guides for Seven Societies*. Cambridge: Cambridge University Press.

Burman, E. (2001) Beyond the baby and the bathwater: post-dualist developmental psychology, *European Early Childhood Education Research Journal*, 9 (1), 5–22.

Burr, R. Children's rights: international policy and lived practice, in M. J. Kehily (ed.) *An Introduction to Childhood Studies* (2nd edn.). Maidenhead: Open University Press, pp. 145–59.

Calder, J. (1994) Occupational health and safety issues for child-care providers, *Pediatrics*, 94 (6), 1072–4.

Caldwell, R. (2007) Agency and change: re-evaluating Foucault's legacy, *Organization*, 14 (6), 1–23.

Cameron, C. (2006) Men in the nursery revisited, *Contemporary Issues in Early Childhood*, 7 (1), 68–79.

Cameron, C., Moss, P. and Owen, C. (1999) *Men in the Nursery: Gender and Caring Work*. London: Sage.

Canella, G.S. (1997) *Deconstructing Early Childhood Education: Social Justice and Revolution. Rethinking Childhood* (Vol. 2). New York: Peter Lang.

Capra, F. (1996). *The Web of Life: A New Scientific Understanding of Living Systems*. New York: Anchor Books.

Carl, B. (2007) *Child Caregiver Interaction Scale*. Dissertation, School of Graduate Studies and Research, Indiana University of Pennsylvania, Indiana, PA.

Carr, D. (2003) *Making Sense of Education: An Introduction to the Philosophy and Theory of Education and Teaching*. London: Routledge.

Carr, W. and Hartnett, A. (1996) *Education and the Struggle for Democracy: The Politics of Educational Ideas*. Maidenhead: Open University Press.

Carroll-Lind, J. (2011) Through their lens: an inquiry into non-parental education and care of infants and toddlers, *The First Years*, 13 (1), 39–44.

Chambless, C. and Jack, T. (2007) *Grandparents as Caregivers in Utah*. Policy Brief, Center for Public Policy and Administration, The University of Utah, Salt Lake City, UT. Available at: www.cppa.utah.edu (accessed 27 March 2012.)

Chanfreau, J., Gowland, S., Lancaster, Z., Poole, E., Tipping, S. and Toomse, M. (2011) *Maternity and Paternity Rights Survey and Women Returners Survey 2009/10*. London: Department for Work and Pensions.

Chang, H.N.-L., Muckelroy, A., Pulido-Tobiassen, D. and Dowell, C. (2000) Redefining childcare and early education in a diverse society: dialogue and reflection, in L.D. Soto (ed.) *The Politics of Early Childhood*. New York: Peter Lang.

Clark, A. and Moss, P. (2001) *Listening to Young Children: The Mosaic Approach*. London: National Children's Bureau.

Clark, A. and Moss, P. (2008) *Spaces to Play: More Listening to Young Children Using the Mosaic Approach*. London: National Children's Bureau.

Clark, A., Kjorholt, A.T. and Moss, P. (2005) *Beyond Listening: Perspectives on Early Childhood Services*. Bristol: Policy Press.

Clark, L. (2009) 1 in 4 middle-class babies in childcare despite warnings it harms children's development, *Daily Mail*, 27 March 2009. Available at: http://www.dailymail.co.uk/news/article–1165157/1-4-middle-class-babies-childcare-despite-warnings-harms-childrens-development.html.

Clarke, G. (2008) *At the Source: A Writer's Year*. Manchester: Carcanet.

Colker, L.J. (2008) Twelve characteristics of effective early childhood teachers, *Young Children*, 63 (2): 68–73.

Colley, H. (2006) Learning to labour with feeling: class, gender and emotion in childcare education and training, *Contemporary Issues in Early Childhood*, 7 (1), 15–29.

Cuthbert, C., Rayns, G. and Stanley, K. (2011) *All Babies Count: Prevention and Protection for Vulnerable Babies*. London: NSPCC.

Dahlberg, G. (2003) Pedagogy as a loci of an ethics of an encounter, in M.N. Bloch, K. Holmlund, I. Moqvist and T.S. Popkewitz (eds.) *Governing Children, Families and Education: Restructuring the Welfare State*. New York: Palgrave Macmillan.

Dahlberg, G. and Moss, P. (2005) *Ethics and Politics in Early Childhood Education*. London: Routledge.

Dalli, C. (2010) Towards the emergence of a critical ecology of the early childhood profession in New Zealand, *Contemporary Issues in Early Childhood*, 11 (1), 61–74.

Dalli, C., White, E.J., Rockel, J., Duhn, I., with Buchanan, E., Davidson, S., Ganly, S., Kus, L. and Wang, B. (2011) *Quality Early Childhood Education for Under-Two-Year-Olds: What Should it Look Like? A Literature Review*. Report to the Ministry of Education. Wellington: Ministry of Education.

Daniel, J. and Shapiro, J. (1996) The infant's transition from home to center-based care, *Child and Youth Care Forum*, 25 (2), 111–23.

Daniel, P. and Ivatts, J. (1998) *Children and Social Policy*. London: Palgrave Macmillan.

Danko-McGhee, K. (2011) The aesthetic responses of babies: paintings that captivate their interest, *NZRECE Journal*, 14, 95–120.

Darling, N. (2007) Ecological systems theory: the person in the center of the circles, *Research in Human Development*, 4 (3/4), 203–17.

David, T. (1996) Researching early childhood: method matters, *International Journal of Early Childhood*, 28 (1), 1–7.

David, T. (1999) *Under Five – Under Educated?* Buckingham: Open University Press.

David, T. (2005) Re-enchanting early childhood?, in D. Hayes (ed.) The *RoutledgeFalmer Guide to Key Debates in Education*. London: RoutledgeFalmer.

David, T. (2009) Young children's social and emotional development, in T. Maynard and N. Thomas (eds.) *An Introduction to Early Childhood Studies* (2nd edn.). London: Sage.

David, T. and Powell, S. (2005) Play in the early years: the influence of cultural difference, in J. Moyles (ed.) *The Excellence of Play* (2nd edn.). Maidenhead: Open University Press.

David, T., Raban, B., Ure, C. Goouch, K., Jago, M., Barriere, I. and Lambirth, A. (2000) *Making Sense of Early Literacy: A Practitioner's Perspective*. Stoke-on-Trent: Trentham Books.

David, T., Goouch, K., Powell, S. and Abbott, L. (2003) *Birth to Three Matters: A Review of the Literature*. Research Report #444. Nottingham: DfES Publications.

Daycare Trust (2009) *Quality Costs: Paying for Early Childhood Education and Care*. London: Daycare Trust.

Dean, H. (2006) *Social Policy*. Cambridge: Polity Press.

Degotardi, S. (2010) High-quality interactions with infants: relationships with early childhood practitioners' interpretations and qualification levels in play and routine contexts, *International Journal of Early Years Education*, 18 (1), 27–41.

Degotardi, S. and Pearson, E. (2009) Relationship theory in the nursery: attachment and beyond, *Contemporary Issues in Early Childhood*, 10 (2), 144–55.

DeMause, L. (1974) *The History of Childhood*. London: Souvenir Press.

Department for Children, Schools and Families (DCSF) (2008) *Statutory Framework for the Early Years Foundation Stage*. Nottingham: DCSF Publications.

Department for Education (DfE) (2011) *Call for Evidence for the Independent Review of Early Education and Childcare Qualifications*. Nottingham: DfE Publications.

Department for Education (DfE) (2012) *Statutory Framework for the Early Years Foundation Stage: Revised Version*. Nottingham: DfE Publications.

Department for Education and Skills (DfES) (2002) *Birth to Three Matters: A Framework to Support Children in their Earliest Years*. Nottingham: DfES Publications.

Dineen, F. (2009) Does relationship training for caregivers enhance young children's learning and language?, in T. Papatheodorou and J. Moyles (eds.) *Learning Together in the Early Years: Exploring Relational Pedagogy*. London: Routledge.

Draper, L. and Wheeler, H. (2010) Working with parents, in B. Duffy and H. Penn (eds.) *Contemporary Issues in the Early Years*. London: Sage.

Duncan, J. (2010) National 'treasures': the Aotearoa New Zealand child, in N. Yelland (ed.) *Contemporary Perspectives on Early Childhood Education*. Maidenhead: Open University Press.

Dunn, J. (1983) Sibling relationships in early childhood, *Child Development*, 54 (4), 787–811.

Dunn, J. (1988) *The Beginnings of Social Understanding*. Oxford: Blackwell.

Dunn, J. (1993) *Young Children's Close Relationships: Beyond Attachment*. London: Sage.

Dunn, J. and Kendrick, C. (1982) *Siblings: Love, Envy and Understanding*. London: Grant McIntyre.

Education, Audiovisual and Culture Executive Agency (EACEA) (2009) *Tackling Social and Cultural Inequalities through Early Childhood Education and Care in Europe*. Brussels: EACEA.

Edwards, C., Gandini, L. and Forman, G. (1998) *The Hundred Languages of Children* (2nd edn.). Greenwich, CT: Ablex.

Eisenstadt, N. (2011) *Providing a Sure Start: How Government Discovered Early Childhood*. Bristol: Policy Press.

Elfer, P. (2005) Observation matters, in L. Abbott and A. Langston (eds.) *Birth to Three Matters*. Maidenhead: Open University Press.

Elfer, P. (2006) Exploring children's expressions of attachment in nursery, *European Early Childhood Education Research Journal*, 14 (2), 81–95.

Elfer, P. (2012) Emotion in nursery work: work discussion as a model of critical professional reflection, *Early Years: An International Journal of Research and Development*, 32 (2), 129–41.

Elfer, P. and Dearnley, K. (2007) Nurseries and emotional well-being: evaluating an emotionally containing model of professional development, *Early Years: An International Journal of Research and Development*, 27 (3), 267–79.

Elfer, P., Goldschmied, E. and Selleck, D. (2003) *Key Persons in Nursery: Building Relationships for Quality Provision*. London: David Fulton.

Elicker, J. and Fortner-Wood, C. (1995) Research in review: adult–child relationships in early childhood programs, *Young Children*, 51 (1), 69–78.

ESF (2008) Final Report. ESF Exploratory Workshop 'Children's participation in decision-making: Exploring theory, policy and practice across Europe', Berlin, 16–18 June.

Evangelou, M., Sylva, K., Kyriakou, M., Wild, M. and Glenny, G. (2009) *Early Years Learning and Development Literature Review*. RR–176. Nottingham: DfE Publications.

Fairclough, N. (1992) *Critical Discourse Analysis*. London: Longman.

Fairclough, N. (2011) Semiotic aspects of social transformation and learning, in R. Rogers (ed.) *An Introduction to Critical Discourse Analysis in Education*. London: Routledge.

Farquhar, S. and Fitzsimons, P. (2008) Introduction, in S. Farquhar and P. Fitzsimons (eds.) *Philosophy of Early Childhood Education*. Oxford: Blackwell.

Fenech, M. (2011) An analysis of the conceptualisation of 'quality' in early childhood education and care empirical research: promoting 'blind spots' as foci for future research, *Contemporary Issues in Early Childhood*, 12 (2), 102–17.

Fenech, M. and Sumsion, J. (2007) Early childhood teachers and regulation: complicating power relations using a Foucauldian lens, *Contemporary Issues in Early Childhood*, 8 (2), 109–22.

Field, F. (2010) *The Foundation Years: Preventing Poor Children Becoming Poor Adults*. London: The Stationery Office.

Field, T. (2007) *The Amazing Infant*. Malden, MA: Blackwell.

Fleer, M. (2005) Developmental fossils – unearthing the artefacts of early childhood education: the reification of child development, *Australian Journal of Early Childhood*, 30 (2), 2–7.

Foster, F. (2012) *The Parent Trap*, ITV1, May 2012.

Foucault, M. (1994) *Discipline and Punish: The Birth of the Prison*. London: Penguin Books.

Frayne, M. (2006) *The Human Touch*. London, Faber & Faber.

Freire, P. (1970) *Pedagogy of the Oppressed* (trans. Myra Bergman Ramos). London: Penguin Books.

Gammage, P. (2006) Early childhood education and care: politics, policies and possibilities, *Early Years: An International Journal of Research and Development*, 26 (3), 235–48.

Gammage, P. (2008) The social agenda and early childhood care and education: can we really help create a better world? *Outline Outreach Paper 4*. The Hague: Bernard van Leer Foundation.

Gerhardt, S. (2004) *Why Love Matters: How Affection Shapes a Baby's Brain*. Hove: Brunner-Routledge.

Giddens, A. (1984) *The Constitution of Society*. London: Macmillan.

Goldschmied, E. and Jackson, S. (1994) *People Under Three: Young Children in Day Care*. London: Routledge.

Goldschmied, E. and Jackson, S. (2004) *People Under Three: Young Children in Day Care* (2nd edn.). London: Routledge.

Goodson, I. and Hargreaves, A. (1996) *Teachers' Professional Lives*. London: Falmer Press.

Goouch, K. (2010) *Towards Excellence in Early Years Education: Exploring Narratives of Experience.* London: Routledge.

Goouch, K. and Powell, S. (2012) Orchestrating professional development for baby room practitioners: raising the stakes in new dialogic encounters, *Journal of Early Childhood Research* DOI: 10.1177/1476 718X12448374.

Gopnik, A. (2009) *The Philosophical Baby.* London: The Bodley Head.

Gopnik, A., Meltzoff, A. and Kuhl, P. (1999) *How Babies Think.* London: Phoenix.

Gove, M. (2011) *The Importance of Early Years*, Speech to the London Early Years Foundation, London, 28 October 2011. Available at: http://www.education.gov.uk/inthenews/speeches/a00199946/michael-gove-speaks-to-the-london-early-years-foundation-about-the-importance-of-early-years (accessed 13 November 2012).

Graham-Matheson, L., Hryniewicz, L., Powell, S., Meehan, P. and Robinson, S. (2009) *Children's Views of their Workforce.* Leeds: Children's Workforce Network.

Greenfield, S. (2000) *The Private Life of the Brain.* London: Penguin Books.

Hall, K. (2001) An analysis of primary literacy policy in England using Barthes' notion of 'readerly' and 'writerly' texts, *Journal of Early Childhood Literacy*, 1 (2), 153–65.

Hargreaves, A. (2000) Four ages of professionalism and professional learning, *Teachers and Teaching: History and Practice*, 6 (2), 151–82.

Härkönen, U. (2007) The Bronfenbrenner ecological systems theory of human development, in *Scientific Articles of V International Conference PERSON.COLOR. NATURE.MUSIC*, 17–21 October, Daugavpils University, Saule, Latvia.

Harris, K. and Wilson, T. (2012) *Baby Room Project.* Chatham: Medway Council.

Heath, S.B. (1983) *Ways with Words: Language, Life and Work in Communities and Classrooms.* Cambridge: Cambridge University Press.

Her Majesty's (HM) Treasury (2004) *Choice for Parents, the Best Start for Children: A Ten-year Strategy for Childcare.* London: The Stationery Office.

Heywood, C. (2010) Centuries of childhood: an anniversary and an epitaph?, *Journal of the History of Childhood and Youth*, 3 (3), 341–65.

Hobson, P. (2002) *The Cradle of Thought: Exploring the Origins of Thinking.* London: Pan Books.

Hohmann, U. (2007) Rights, expertise and negotiations in care and education, *Early Years: An International Journal of Research and Development*, 27 (1), 33–46.

Hopkins, J. (1988) Facilitating the development of intimacy between nurses and infants in day nurseries. *Early Child Development and Care*, 33 (1–4), 99–111.

Howes, C. and Ritchie, S. (2002) *A Matter of Trust: Connecting Teachers and Learners in the Early Childhood Classroom.* New York: Teachers College Press.

Huitt, W. (2011). *Analyzing Paradigms Used in Education and Schooling.* Educational Psychology Interactive. Valdosta, GA: Valdosta State University. Available at: http://www.edpsycinteractive.org/topics/intro/paradigm.html (accessed 13 November 2012).

Hunt, S., Virgo, S., Klett-Davies, M., Page, A. and Apps, J. (2011) *Provider Influence on the Early Home Learning Environment (EHLE)*. RR–142. Nottingham: DfE Publications.

Inglis, D. and Thorpe, C. (2012) *An Invitation to Social Theory*. Cambridge: Polity Press.

James, O. (2010) *The Pros and Cons of Day Care*. Available at: http://www.selfishcapitalist.com/docs/HOW%20Not%20Extract%20w%20Biblio. pdf accessed 13 November 2012).

Jelicic, H., Theokas, C., Phelps, E. and Lerner, R.M. (2007) Conceptualizing and measuring the context within person ↔ (context models of human development: implications for theory, research and application, in T.D. Little, J.A. Bovaird and N.A. Card (eds.) *Modelling Contextual Effects in Longitudinal Studies*. Mahwah, NJ: Lawrence Erlbaum.

Johnson, E.M. (2012) Women and children first, *Times Higher Education*, 15 March. Available at: www.timeshighereducation.co.uk/story.asp?storycode=419301 (accessed 13 November 2012).

Jones, P. (2011) What are children's rights? Contemporary developments and debates, in P. Jones and G. Walker (eds.) *Children's Rights in Practice*. London: Sage.

Kaga, Y., Bennett, J. and Moss, P. (2010) *Caring and Learning Together: A Cross National Study on the Integration of Early Childhood Care and Education within Education*. Paris: UNESCO.

Karmiloff-Smith, A. (1994) *Baby it's You*. London: Ebury Press.

Karmiloff, K. and Karmiloff-Smith, A. (2001) *Pathways to Language: From Fetus to Adolescent*. Cambridge, MA: Harvard University Press.

Kehily, M. (ed.) (2008) *An Introduction to Childhood Studies* (2nd edn.). Maidenhead: Open University Press.

Kernan, M. and Singer, E. (eds.) (2011) *Peer Relationships in Early Childhood Education and Care*. London: Routledge.

Keyser, J. (2006) *From Parents to Partners: Building a Family-centered Early Childhood Program*. St. Paul, MN: Redleaf Press.

Kjørholt, A.T. (2011) Rethinking young children's rights for participation in diverse cultural contexts, in M. Kernan and E. Singer (eds.) *Peer Relationships in Early Childhood Education and Care*. London: Routledge, 38–48.

Kottelenberg, M. and Lehrer, S.F. (2011) *Reinvestigating Who Benefits and Who Loses from Universal Childcare in Canada*. Queen's University, Kingston, Ontario, Canada.

Kress, G. (2012) Discourse analysis and education: a multimodal semiotic approach, in R. Rogers (ed.) *An Introduction to Critical Discourse Analysis in Education* (2nd edn.). London: Routledge.

Kuhl, P. and Meltzoff, A. (1996) Infant vocalisations in response to speech: vocal imitation and developmental change, *Journal of the Acoustical Society of America*, 100 (4), 2425–38.

Kuhn, T.S. (1996) *The Structure of Scientific Revolutions* (3rd edn.). Chicago, IL: University of Chicago Press.

Laevers, F. (1997) *A Process-Orientated Child Follow-up System for Young Children.* Leuven: Center for Experiential Education, Leuven University.

Langston, A. (2012) Back to basics, *Nursery World,* 11–24 June, pp. 19–22.

Lash, M. and McMullen, M. (2008) The child care trilemma: how moral orientations influence the field, *Contemporary Issues in Early Childhood,* 9 (1), 36–48.

Leach, P. (2012) Birth to threes: babies are people, *Nursery World,* 7 February.

Lerner, R.M. (2005) Foreword, in U. Bronfenbrenner, *Making Human Beings Human: Bioecological Perspectives on Human Development.* London: Sage.

Levin, P. (1997) *Making Social Policy: The Mechanisms of Government and Politics, and How to Investigate Them.* Buckingham: Open University Press.

Lewis, C. (2010) John Newson Obituary, *The Guardian,* 14 June. Available at: http://www.guardian.co.uk/science/2010/jun/14/john-newson-obituary (accessed 13 November 2012).

Lewis, J. (2009) *Work–Family Balance, Gender and Policy.* Cheltenham: Edward Elgar.

Lowe, R. (2009) Childhood through the ages, in T. Maynard and N.P. Thomas (eds.) *An Introduction to Early Childhood Studies* (2nd edn.). London: Sage.

Lynch, K. (2007) Love labour as a distinct and non-commodifiable form of care labour, *The Sociological Review,* 55 (3), 551–70.

MacNaughton, G. (2003) *Shaping Early Childhood: Learners, Curriculum and Contexts.* Maidenhead: Open University Press.

MacNaughton, G. and Smith, K. (2009) Children's rights in early childhood, in M.J. Kehily (ed.) *An Introduction to Childhood Studies* (2nd edn.). Maidenhead: Open University Press.

Malaguzzi, L. (1998) History, ideas and basic philosophy, in C. Edwards, L. Gandini and G. Forman (eds.) *The Hundred Languages of Children* (2nd edn.). Greenwich, CT: Ablex.

Manning-Morton, J. (2006) The personal is professional: professionalism and the birth to threes practitioner, *Contemporary Issues in Early Childhood,* 7 (1), 42–52.

Manning-Morton, J. and Thorp, M. (2003) *Key Times for Play: The First Three Years.* Maidenhead: Open University Press.

Mantzavinos, C. (2009) *Naturalistic Hermeneutics.* Cambridge: Cambridge University Press.

Martins, C. and Gaffan, E.A. (2000) Effects of early maternal depression on patterns of infant–mother attachment: a meta-analytic investigation, *Journal of Child Psychology and Psychiatry,* 41, 737–46.

Mathers, S., Singler, R. and Karemaker, A. (2012) *Improving Quality in the Early Years: A Comparison of Perspectives and Measures.* Available at: http://www.education.ox.ac.uk/research/fell/research/improving-quality-in-the-early-years/ (accessed 13 November 2012).

McHale, J.P. (2007) When infants grow up in multiperson relationship systems, *Infant Mental Health Journal,* 28 (4), 370–92.

McMullen, M.B., Addleman, J.M., Fulford, A.M., Moore, S.L., Mooney, S.J., Sisk, S.S. and Zachariah, J. (2009) Learning to be me while coming to understand we: encouraging prosocial babies in group settings, *Young Children*, 64 (4), 20–8.

Medwell, J., Wray, D., Poulson, L. and Fox, R. (1998) *Effective Teachers of Literacy: A Report of a Research Project Commissioned by the Teacher Training Agency*. Exeter: University of Exeter.

Meggitt, C. (2001) *Baby and Child Health*. Oxford: Heinemann.

Miller, L. and Hevey, D. (2012) *Policy Issues in the Early Years*. London: Sage.

Moje, E.B., Ciechanowski, K.M., Kramer, K., Ellis, L., Carrillo, R. and Collazo, T. (2004) Working toward third space in content area literacy: an examination of everyday funds of knowledge and discourse, *Reading Research Quarterly*, 39 (1), 38–70.

Mooney, A. and Blackburn, T. (2003) *Children's Views on Childcare Quality*. RR 482. Nottingham: DfES Publications.

Mooney, A. and Munton, A.G. (1998) Quality in early childhood services: parent, provider and policy perspectives, *Children and Society*, 12, 101–12.

Moss, P. (2001) The otherness of Reggio, in L. Abbot and C. Nutbrown (eds.) *Experiencing Reggio Emilia: Implications for Prechool provision*. Buckingham: Open University Press, pp. 125–37.

Moss, P. (2006) Structures, understandings and discourses: possibilities for re-envisioning the early childhood worker, *Contemporary Issues in Early Childhood*, 7 (1), 30–41.

Moss, P. (2008) Meeting across the paradigmatic divide, in S. Farquhar and P. Fitzsimons (eds.) *Philosophy of Early Childhood Education*. Oxford: Blackwell.

Mouffe, C. (2000) *The Democratic Paradox*. London: Verso.

Mozere, L. (2008) In early childhood: what's language about?, in S Farquhar and P Fitzsimons (eds.) *Philosophy of Early Childhood Education*. Oxford: Blackwell.

Mukherji, P. and Albon, D. (2010) *Research Methods in Early Childhood: An Introductory Guide*. London: Sage.

Murray, L. and Andrews, L. (2000) *The Social Baby*. Richmond, Surrey: CP Publishing.

National Institute of Child Health and Human Development (NICHD) (1998) Early child care and self-control, compliance, and problem behavior at twenty-four and thirty-six months: the NICHD Early Child Care Research Network, *Child Development*, 69 (4), 1145–70.

National Institute of Child Health and Human Development (NICHD) (2000) The relation of child care to cognitive and language development: National Institute of Child Health and Human Development Early Child Care Research Network, *Child Development*, 71 (4), 960–80.

National Institute of Child Health and Human Development (NICHD) (2001) Child care and children's peer interaction at 24 and 36 months: the NICHD Study of Early Child Care, *Child Development*, 72 (5), 1478–500.

Neale, B. and Smart, C. (1998) *Agents or Dependants? Struggling to Listen to Children in Family Law and Family Research*, Working Paper #3. Leeds: Centre for Research on Family, Kinship and Childhood.

Newson, E. and Newson, J. (1979) *Toys and Playthings*. London: Penguin Books.

Newson, J. and Newson, E. (1963) *Infant Care in an Urban Community*. Harmondsworth: Pelican Books.

Newson, J. and Newson, E. (1968) *Four Years Old in an Urban Community* (2nd edn.). London: Allen & Unwin.

Newson, J. and Newson, E. (1976) *Seven Years Old in the Home Environment*. Harmondsworth: Pelican Books.

Newson, J. and Newson, E. (1977) *Perspectives on School at Seven Years Old*. London: Allen & Unwin.

Nias, J. (1989) *Primary Teachers Talking: A Study of Teaching as Work*. London: Routledge.

Noddings, N. (1984) *Caring: A Feminine Approach to Ethics and Moral Education*. Berkeley, CA: University of California Press.

Nutbrown, C. (2012a) *Foundations for Quality: Review of Early Childhood Qualifications*. Available at: http://www.education.gov.uk/nutbrownreview (accessed 13 November 2012).

Nutbrown, C. (2012b) *Review of Early Education and Childcare Qualifications*. Interim Report, March. London: DfE.

Nutbrown, C. and Page, J. (2008) *Working with Babies and Children from Birth to Three*. London: Sage.

NV2 Courses Hub (2012) *NVQ Courses Information Hub* http://www.nvqcourse-shub.co.uk/ (accessed 13 November 2012).

Oates, R. and Sanders, A. (2009) Making a little difference for early childhood studies students, in T. Papatheodoru and J. Moyles (eds.) *Learning Together in the Early Years: Exploring Relational Pedagogy*. London: Routledge.

Office for National Statistics (2000) *Standard Occupational Classification 2000, Vol. 1: Structure and Descriptions of Unit Groups*. London: The Stationery Office.

Olssen, M., Codd, J. and O'Neill, A.-M. (2004) *Education Policy: Globalization, Citizenship and Democracy*. London: Sage.

Organization for Economic Cooperation and Development (OECD) (2001) *Starting Strong: Early Childhood Education and Care*. Paris: OECD.

Organization for Economic Cooperation and Development (OECD) (2006) *Starting Strong II: Early Childhood Education and Care*. Paris: OECD.

Organization for Economic Cooperation and Development (OECD) (2011) *PF2.1: Key Characteristics of Parental Leave Systems*. Social Policy Division – Directorate of Employment, Labour and Social Affairs. OECD Family Database. Available at: www.oecd.org/els/social/family/database (accessed 13 November 2012).

Organization for Economic Cooperation and Development (OECD) (2012) *Quality Matters in Early Childhood Education and Care: United Kingdom (England) 2012*. Paris: OECD Publishing.

Osgood, J. (2005) Who cares? The classed nature of childcare, *Gender and Education*, 17 (3), 289–303.

Osgood, J. (2006) Deconstructing professionalism in the early years: resisting the regulatory gaze, *Contemporary Issues in Early Childhood*, 7 (1), 5–14.

Osgood, J. (2010) Reconstructing professionalism in ECEC: the case for the 'critically reflective emotional professional', *Early Years: An International Journal of Research and Development*, 30 (2), 119–33.

Osgood, J. (2012) *Narratives from the Nursery: Negotiating Professional Identities in Early Childhood*. London: Routledge.

Owen, T.M., Ware, A.M. and Barfoot, B. (2000). Caregiver–mother partnership behaviour and the quality of caregiver–child and mother–child interactions, *Early Childhood Research Quarterly*, 15 (3), 413–28.

Ozga, J. (2000) *Policy Research in Educational Settings: Contested Terrain*. Buckingham: Open University Press.

Page, J. (2011) Do mothers want professional carers to love their babies?, *Journal of Early Childhood Research*, 9 (3), 310–23.

Peeters, J. (2008) *The Construction of a New Profession*. Amsterdam: SWP.

Penn, H. (2008) *Understanding Early Childhood: Issues and Controversies* (2nd edn.). Maidenhead: Open University Press.

Powell, S. (2010) Hide and seek: values in early childhood education and care policies, *British Journal of Educational Studies*, 58 (2), 213–29.

Powell, S. and Goouch, K. (2012) Whose hand rocks the cradle? Parallel discourses in the baby room, *Early Years: An International Journal of Research and Development*, 32(2), 113–27.

Pugh, G. (2010) The policy agenda for early childhood services, in G. Pugh and B. Duffy (eds.) *Contemporary Issues in the Early Years*. London: Sage.

Puroila, A.-M. and Karila, K. (2001) Bronfenbrenner in ekologinen teoria [Bronfenbrenner's ecological theory], in K. Karila, J. Kinos and J. Virtanen (eds.) *Varhaiskasvatuksen teoriasuuntauksia* [*Theoretical Approaches in Early Childhood Education*]. Jyväskylä: PS-Kustannus.

Raikes, H. (1996) A secure base for babies: applying attachment concepts to the infant care setting, *Young Children*, 51 (5), 59–67.

Recchia, S.L. (2012) Caregiver–child relationships as a context for continuity in child care, *Early Years: An International Journal of Research and Development*, 32 (2), 143–57.

Reifsnider, E., Gallagher, M. and Forgione, B. (2005) Using ecological models in research on health disparities, *Journal of Professional Nursing*, 21 (4), 216–22.

Rentzou, K. (2011) Parent–caregiver relationship dyad in Greek day care centres, *International Journal of Early Years Education*, 19 (2), 163–77.

Rice, W.R., Gavrilets, S. and Friberg, U. (2010) The evolution of sex-specific grandparental harm, *Proceedings of the Royal Society of London B: Biological Sciences*, 277 (1694), 2727–35.

Richards, M. (1998) The meeting of nature and nurture and the development of children: some conclusions, in C. Panter-Brick (ed.) *Biosocial Perspectives on Children*. Cambridge: Cambridge University Press.

Rinaldi, C. (2005) *In Dialogue with Reggio Emilia: Listening, Researching, and Learning*. Abingdon: Routledge.

Roberts, R. (2010) *Wellbeing from Birth*. London: Sage.

Robinson, K. and Jones Díaz, C. (2006) *Diversity and Difference in Early Childhood Education: Issues for Theory and Practice*. Maidenhead: Open University Press.

Robinson, M. (2003) *From Birth to One: The Year of Opportunity*. Maidenhead: Open University Press.

Robinson, M. (2008) *Child Development 0–8: A Journey Through the Early Years*. Maidenhead: Open University Press.

Rockel, J. (2009) A pedagogy of care: moving beyond the margins of managing work and minding babies, *Australasian Journal of Early Childhood*, 34 (3), 1–8.

Rockel, J. and Craw, J. (2011) Discourses of happiness in infant–toddler pedagogy, *NZRECE Journal*, 14, 121–31.

Rogoff, B. (1990) *Apprenticeship in Thinking: Cognitive Development in Social Context*. Oxford: Oxford University Press.

Sammons, P., Elliot, K., Sylva, K., Melhuish, E., Siraj-Blatchford, I. and Taggart, B. (2004) The impact of pre-school on young children's cognitive attainments at entry to reception, *British Educational Research Journal*, 30 (5), 691–712.

Save the Children/Daycare Trust (2012) *Making Work Pay – The Childcare Trap*. London: Save the Children.

Shanghai Municipal Government (2007) *Three-Year (2006–2008) Action Program of Shanghai Municipality for Pre-school Education*. Shanghai: Shanghai Municipal Government.

Simpson, G. and Connor, S. (2011) *Social Policy for Social Welfare Professionals: Tools for Understanding, Analysis and Engagement*. Bristol: Policy Press.

Singer, E. and de Haan, D. (2007) *The Social Lives of Young Children*. Amsterdam: SWP.

Siraj-Blatchford, I. and Clarke, P. (2000) *Supporting Identity, Diversity and Language in the Early Years*. Maidenhead: Open University Press.

Siraj-Blatchford, I. and Sylva, K. (2004) Researching pedagogy in English pre-schools, *British Educational Research Journal*, 30 (5), 713–30.

Small, M. (1998) *Our Babies, Ourselves: How Biology and Culture Shape the Way We Parent*. New York: Anchor Books.

Smith, C.A. (2006) *Grandparents as Caregivers: Heartbreak and Hope*. Manhattan, KS: Kansas State University. Available at: www.ksre.ksu.edu/library/famlf2/mf2744.pdf (accessed 27 March 2012).

Smith, F. (1992) *To Think*. London: Routledge.

Smith, R., Poole, E., Perry, J., Wollny, I., Reeves, J., with Coshall, C. and d'Souza, J. (2010) *Childcare and Early Years Survey of Parents 2009*. Nottingham: DCSF Publications.

Soto, L.D. (ed.) (2000) *The Politics of Early Childhood Education*. New York: Peter Lang.

Stefansen, K. and Skogen, K. (2010) Selective identification, quiet distancing: understanding the working-class response to the Nordic daycare model, *The Sociological Review*, 58 (4), 588–603.

Stern, D. (1977) *The First Relationship: Infant and Mother*. London: Fontana.

Stones, R. (2005) *Structuration Theory*. Basingstoke: Palgrave Macmillan.

Stones, R. (ed.) (2007) *Key Sociological Thinkers* (2nd edn.). London: Palgrave Macmillan.

Stronach, I., Corbin, B., McNamara, O., Stark, S. and Warne, T. (2002) Towards an uncertain politics of professionalism: teacher and nurser identities in flux, *Journal of Education Policy*, 17 (1), 109–38.

Sunderland, M. (2006) *The Science of Parenting*. London: Dorling Kindersley.

Super, C.M. and Harkness, S. (1998) The development of affect in infancy and early childhood, in M. Woodhead, D. Faulkner and K. Littleton (eds.) *Cultural Worlds of Early Childhood*. London: Routledge.

Swadener, B.B. and Lubeck, S. (1995) *Children and Families 'At Promise'. Deconstructing the Discourse of Risk*. New York: State University of New York Press.

Swick, K.J. and Williams, R.D. (2006) An analysis of Bronfenbrenner's bio-ecological perspective for early childhood educators: implications for working with families experiencing stress, *Early Childhood Education Journal*, 33 (5), 371–8.

Sylva, K. and Roberts, F. (2010) Quality in early childhood education: evidence for long-term effects, in G. Pugh and B. Duffy (eds.) *Contemporary Issues in the Early Years* (5th edn.). London: Sage.

Taguchi, H.L. (2010a) Rethinking pedagogical practices in early childhood education: a multidimensional approach to learning and inclusion, in N. Yelland (ed.) *Contemporary Perspectives on Early Childhood Education*. Maidenhead: McGraw-Hill.

Taguchi, H.L. (2010b) *Going Beyond the Theory/Practice Divide in Early Childhood Education: Introducing an Intra-active Pedagogy*. London: Routledge.

Teti, D.M., Gelfand, D.M., Messenger, D.S. and Russell, I. (1995) Maternal depression and the quality of early attachment: an examination of infants, preschoolers, and their mothers. *Developmental Psychology*, 31 (3), 364–76.

Tickell, C. (2011) *The Early Years: Foundations for Life, Health and Learning. An Independent Report on the Early Years Foundation Stage to Her Majesty's Government*. London: DfES.

Tolkien, J.R.R. (2009) *The Hobbit*. London: HarperCollins.

Trevarthen, C. (1998) The child's need to learn a culture, in M. Woodhead, D. Faulkner and K. Littlejohn (eds.) *Cultural Worlds of Early Childhood*. London: Routledge.

Trevarthen, C. and Aitken, K.J. (2001) Infant intersubjectivity: research, theory, and clinical applications, *Journal of Child Psychology and Psychiatry and Allied Disciplines*, 42 (1), 3–48.

Trevarthen, C., Barr, I., Dunlop, A.-W., Gjersoe, N., Marwick, H. and Stephen, C. (2003) *Supporting a Young Child's Needs for Care and Affection, Shared Meaning and a Social Place. Review of Childcare and the Development of Children Aged 0–3: Research Evidence, and Implications for Out-of-Home Provision.* Edinburgh: Scottish Executive. Available at: http://www.scotland.gov.uk/Resource/Doc/933/0007610.pdf (accessed 13 November 2012).

Tveit, A.D. (2009) A parental voice: parents as equal and dependent – rhetoric about parents, teachers, and their conversations, *Educational Review*, 61 (3), 289–300.

United Nations (1989) *Convention on the Rights of the Child.* Geneva: United Nations.

United Nations Children's Fund (UNICEF) (2008) *The Child Care Transition.* Innocenti Report Card 8, 2008. Florence: UNICEF Innocenti Research Centre.

United Nations Educational, Scientific and Cultural Organization (UNESCO) (2007) *Strong Foundations: Early Childhood Education and Care.* EFA Global Monitoring Report 2007 (2nd revised edition). Paris: UNESCO.

Vaughan, G. and Estola, E. (2008) The Gift Paradigm in Early Childhood Education, in S. Farquhar and P. Fitzsimons (eds.) *Philosophy of Early Childhood Education.* Oxford: Blackwell.

Vincent, C. and Ball, S.J. (2001) A market in love? Choosing pre-school childcare, *British Educational Research Journal*, 27 (5), 633–51.

Vincent, C. and Ball, S.J. (2006) *Childcare, Choice and Class Practices: Middle-class Parents and Their Children.* Abingdon: Routledge.

Vincent, C. and Braun, A. (2011) 'I think a lot of it is common sense . . .': early years students, professionalism and the development of a 'vocational habitus', *Journal of Education Policy*, 26 (6), 771–85.

Volosinov, V.N. (1973) *Marxism and the Philosophy of Language.* Cambridge, MA: Harvard University Press.

Vygotsky, L.S. (1986) *Thought and Language.* Cambridge, MA: MIT Press.

Waller, M.R. (2009) Family man in the other America: new opportunities, motivations and supports for paternal caregiving, *Annals of the American Academy of Political and Social Science*, 624, 156–76.

Waxman, S.R. (2002) Early word-learning and conceptual development: everything had a name and each name gave birth to a new thought, in U. Goswami (ed.) *Blackwell Handbook of Cognitive Development.* Oxford: Blackwell.

Weir, R.H. (1962) *Language in the Crib.* The Hague: Mouton.

Whalley, M. and the Pen Green Team (2001) *Involving Parents in their Children's Learning.* London: Paul Chapman.

Whitehead, M. (2009) *Language and Literacy Development in the Early Years* (2nd edn.). Maidenhead: Open University Press.

Woodhead, M., Faulkner, D. and Littleton, K. (eds.) (1998) *Cultural Worlds of Early Childhood.* Maidenhead, Open University Press.

Yeats, W.B. (1994) *Among School Children: The Collected Poems of W.B. Yeats.* Ware: Wordsworth Editions Ltd.

Yelland, N. (ed.) (2005) *Critical Issues in Early Childhood Education.* Maidenhead: Open University Press.

Index

Locators shown in *italics* refer to figures.

A–Z OF PLAY IN EARLY CHILDHOOD

Janet Moyles

9780335246380 (Paperback)
2012

eBook also available

This indispensable guide uses a unique glossary format to explore
some of the key themes in play in early childhood, many of which
regularly arise for students, tutors, parents and practitioners. As
well as covering key concepts, theories and influential figures in the
field, the book considers important aspects of each construct and
highlights the complexity of play in early childhood.

Key features:

- Split into a comprehensive glossary running through elements
  of play from A–Z, it is a useful, fun and unique companion to
  understanding children's play
- Original thoughts from well known early years people including
  Tricia David, Carol Aubrey, Angela Anning and Lilian Katz

www.openup.co.uk

 OPEN UNIVERSITY PRESS
McGraw - Hill Education

GEORGESON & PAYLER

Jan Georgeson and Jane Payler

9780335245918 (Paperback)
February 2013

eBook also available

There is a growing interest in understanding how early years care and education is organised and experienced internationally. This book examines key influential approaches to early years care as well as some less well-known systems from around the world.

Key features:

- Informs those studying early years about perspectives in other countries
- Encourages critical thinking about issues, influences and the complexities of early years provision around the world
- Promotes critical reflection on students' own provision and the current context of that provision

www.openup.co.uk

 OPEN UNIVERSITY PRESS
McGraw - Hill Education

THE ROLE OF THE ADULT IN EARLY YEARS SETTINGS

Janet Rose and Sue Rogers

9780335242306 (Paperback)
July 2012

eBook also available

This essential book focuses on the adult role within early years education and care. The book introduces the concept of the 'plural practitioner', which acknowledges that the role of the adult in early years settings is complex and entails many different responsibilities.

Key features:

- Discussion of the seven different dimensions of the adult role - to help practitioners reflect on the multiple and complex ways in which they work with young children
- Key questions at the end of each chapter to stimulate further reflection and reading
- Case study examples of real practitioner experiences

www.openup.co.uk

 OPEN UNIVERSITY PRESS
McGraw - Hill Education

SAFEGUARDING BABIES AND YOUNG CHILDREN
A Guide for Early Years Professionals

John Powell and Elaine Uppal

9780335234080 (Paperback)
2012

eBook also available

This practical and challenging book focuses on the relationship that early years professionals have with babies, young children and their families/carers. Powell and Uppal reprioritize practice in safeguarding and child protection, and emphasizing the importance of focusing on the skills needed to work successfully in this arena.

Key features:

- Highly practical discussion about safeguarding babies and young children
- A brief history and overview of a number of issues and their relevance for practice
- Case studies allowing the reader to rehearse their possible approaches to a particular scenario

www.openup.co.uk

OBSERVATION
Origins and Approaches in Early
Childhood

Valerie Podmore and Paulette Luff

9780335244249 (Paperback)
2012

eBook also available

"This book is an excellent resource for all those studying or
working in the field of early childhood. It deals with key issues
of observational processes offering a balance between theory
and practical activities. It is written in a critical, engaging and
informative way, with scope for interesting discussions with
students, and is a useful tool for lecturers and students as in
learning about observations for all involved in early childhood
education."
Dr. Ioanna Palaiologou, Lecturer, University of Hull, UK

Key features:

- An adaptation of a book that has been successful in New
  Zealand – updated with UK content
- Rich in examples, drawing on a variety of studies, policies and
  contexts to illustrate key points
- A range of practical techniques, both qualitative and quantitative
  for practitioners

www.openup.co.uk

OPEN UNIVERSITY PRESS
McGraw - Hill Education